COMPUTE!'s
Mastering
MultiMate
Advantage II™

Robert Wolenik

COMPUTE! Books

Greensboro, North Carolina
Radnor, Pennsylvania

Edited by Jill Champion

Printed in the United States of America

10 9 8 7 6 5 4 3 2 1

Library of Congress Cataloging-in-Publication Data
Wolenik, Robert.
    Compute!'s mastering MultiMate Advantage II / Robert Wolenik.
        p.   cm.
    Includes index.
    ISBN 0-87455-154-4
        1. MultiMate Advantage (Computer program) 2. Word processing.
    I. Mastering MultiMate Advantage II.   II. Title.
    Z52.5.M85W64   1988
    652'.5—dc19   88—20409
                                                         CIP

The author and publisher have made every effort in the preparation of this book to ensure the accuracy of the programs and information. However, the information in this book is sold without warranty, either express or implied. Neither the author nor COMPUTE! Publications, Inc. will be liable for any damages caused or alleged to be caused directly, indirectly, incidentally, or consequentially by the programs or information in this book.

The opinions expressed in this book are solely those of the author and are not necessarily those of COMPUTE! Publications, Inc.

COMPUTE! Books, Post Office Box 5406, Greensboro, NC 27403, (919) 275-9809, is a Capital Cities/ABC, Inc. company and is not associated with any manufacturer of personal computers.

MultiMate Advantage II is a trademark of MultiMate International Corporation.

IBM, AT, and PC/XT are registered trademarks of International Business Machines Corporation.

Contents

Preface

This book is useful to both beginning and experienced users of *MultiMate*. If you're a novice, *COMPUTE!'s Mastering MultiMate Advantage II* will get you started quickly and easily. If you're already experienced with *MultiMate,* this book will quickly boost you to top performance and efficiency.

COMPUTE!'s Mastering MultiMate Advantage II looks at this best-selling program by Ashton-Tate from both basic and advanced perspectives.

At its most basic level, *MultiMate Advantage II* is quick to learn, easy to use, and is ideal for simple tasks such as writing letters and addressing envelopes. (Those of you who've used the Wang word processing system will immediately be at ease with this program. Most of the controls are identical to Wang.)

By using this book, even those unfamiliar with word processing can learn the most basic *MultiMate* functions in a matter of minutes.

On the other hand, if you're interested in more involved word processing, *MultiMate Advantage II* provides all the power you need.

And if you're a power user, upgrading from an earlier version of *MultiMate,* or switching from another word processor, the latter chapters (Part II) will help ease you into *MultiMate Advantage II*'s true word processing capabilities.

Introduction

MultiMate Advantage II is one of the world's most sophisticated word processing programs, offering you the ability to quickly transform your ideas into professional looking documents.

It contains specific features not found in many other word processors, including

- A print merge that allows you to use lists generated by other programs to create mailings.
- Graphics for drawing lines of different widths and textures onscreen to create boxes and other graphic effects.
- A true WYSIWYG (What You See Is What You Get) column mode that allows you to generate up to eight columns on a single page, both in snakelike fashion (as found in a phone book or newsletter) or in bound format (where each column contains independent text).
- A Spell Checker and Thesaurus to help you with spellings and correct usages of words.
- Complete printer support so you can run dot-matrix, impact head, and the latest laser jets for basic desktop publishing.
- The ability to organize document files in a variety of formats, placing headers, footers, footnotes, and other specialized text precisely where you want it.

About the Program

MultiMate Advantage II requires you to use an IBM PC/XT/AT or clone with at least 384K of RAM. You may use the program with either a double disk drive or a hard disk. You may also use either 3½-inch or 5¼-inch floppy disks (both are included in the package).

These are the minimum requirements, however. To get the most out of *MultiMate Advantage II*, it's recommended that the program be used with at least 512K RAM and a hard disk—preferably, at least 20 megabytes. Additionally, a color graphics card and color monitor will present the program onscreen in color, which will visually enhance your use of it.

IBM Clones

A special word about IBM clones. Since all IBM clones are incompatible to some extent, you may run into compatibility problems when trying to use *MultiMate Advantage II*. The less compatible the computer, the more likely it is you won't be able to run some of *MultiMate*'s features; therefore, it's suggested that you first try out the software on the hardware with all the programs included in *MultiMate Advantage II*.

Part I

An Introduction to *MultiMate Advantage II*

Chapter 1
Getting Started

Nobody likes taking the time to learn how to use a word processor. We all have important letters, reports, and documents that need to be created immediately, and any time spent learning a program is time away from our work. Getting the basics out of the way is something we all want to do as quickly and painlessly as possible, which is the purpose of Part I of *COMPUTE!'s Mastering MultiMate Advantage II*.

If you're totally new to *MultiMate Advantage II*, you'll find what you need here to get up and running in no time. If you're an experienced user, you'll find this section to be a handy reference for those commands you haven't yet fully committed to memory.

Opening a Document

MultiMate Advantage II allows for two methods of opening a document, *Hot Start* and the normal procedure. Hot Start takes you directly from the DOS prompt to the document. It does not, however, allow for any initial modification of the defaults, nor does it call up the Document Summary screen. Hot Start is best used when you want to edit a document you previously created, or when you want to quickly get going and are willing to accept the previously established defaults.

Hot Start

- From the C> prompt type *wp Name*.
- You may type *wp* in either uppercase or lowercase.
- *Name* refers to the name of the document you're creating. It can be up to eight characters long and have a three-character extension (FIRSTNAM.DOC).
- Path may be inserted between *wp* and *Name* if you wish to have the document created on a different directory (wp C:\DATA\ LETTERS\FIRSTNAM.DOC).

Normal Opening

- From the C> prompt, type *mm*. This will bring you to the *MultiMate Advantage II* main menu.
- To open a previously created document, press 1.
- To open a new document, press 2.

Document Name Screen

This screen asks for the name of the document you're creating or reopening.

- Type the drive (C).
- Type the path (\DATA\LETTERS\).
- Type the document name (FIRSTNAM.DOC).

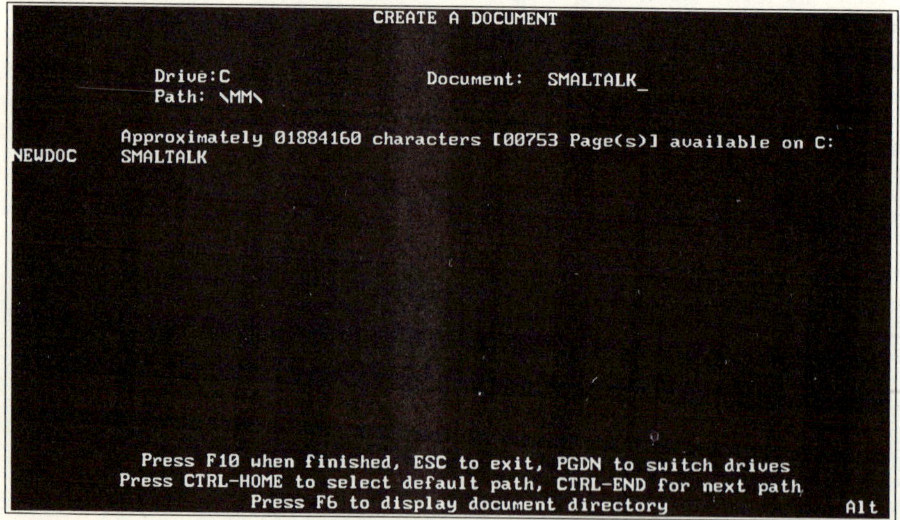

Figure 1-1. Document Name Screen

Document Summary Screen

This screen provides information summarizing the document's contents. You may either enter the information requested or bypass the screen by pressing the F10 key.

Modify Document Defaults

This screen gives the basic defaults that will apply to the document. You may accept the defaults and bypass the screen by pressing F10, or you may change the given defaults.

```
                       MODIFY DOCUMENT DEFAULTS

Allow Widows And Orphans?                Y    Acceptable Decimal Tab [. or ,]?      .
Automatic Page Breaks?                   Y    Number Of Lines Per Page?            55
Backup Before Edit Document?             N    Display Document Startup Screens?     Y
(P)age Or (T)ext Associated Headers And Footers?                                    P

Print Date Standard [(D)OS,(U)SA,(E)urope or (J)apan]?                              D
Currency Symbol              ·   $              (F)ootnotes or (E)ndnotes?          F

Section Numbering Style [(R)oman or (N)umeric]?                                     R




                      Press F10 when finished, ESC to exit              Alt
```

Figure 1-2. Modify Document Defaults Screen

Allow Widows And Orphans? A *widow* is the first line of a paragraph left at the bottom of the page; an *orphan* is the last line of a paragraph at the top of the next page. Professional-looking documents do not contain widows and orphans; however, for informal documents, they're acceptable. The default is *Yes*.

Automatic Page Breaks? *Yes* tells the program you want page breaks automatically inserted. *No* allows you to insert them manually.

Note: Once an automatic page break is inserted, any additional lines typed on that page will not be carried over to the following pages, regardless of the line length specified. Rather, they will be added to the page on which they are typed to a maximum of 195 lines. To reform the page to the designated line length you must "repaginate" (See Chapter 2).

Backup Before Edit Document? Some word processors (such as *WordStar*) automatically back up each document created. *MultiMate Advantage II* gives you the option of creating a backup file. If you select *Yes*, only the latest version used will be backed up.

(P)age or (T)ext Associated Headers And Footers? If you have headers and footers when you repaginate, do you want them linked to the (T)ext where they originally appeared, or do you want them to remain with the (P)age on which they were originally typed? The default (P) will keep them in their most commonly used position.

Acceptable Decimal Tab [. or ,] ? You may choose to use a comma as the decimal indicator. A period is given as the default.

Number Of Lines Per Page? You may choose up to 199 lines per page. However, since *MultiMate Advantage II* thinks of each page as data within a field, the number of lines is related to the length of the line. If you use the line length of 75 characters, the maximum number of lines you can have on a page is roughly 75. If you want the printed document to be double-spaced, (see "Changing the Format" in Chapter 2), just multiply the number of lines you want and type it in. For example, to end up with 24 printed lines on the page, type 48 here.

Display Document Startup Screens? The default is *Yes* and will display the startup screens, which may be useful in a multiple-user system. If you're a single user, you may want to change the default to *No*.

If you enter the date automatically, using the 04/29/1988 command, it can be presented in one of four formats:

DOS:	Month/Day/Year
U.S.A:	Month/Day/Year
European:	Day
Japanese:	Day:Month:Year

Currency Symbol: You can enter any symbol you want. The dollar sign ($) is standard and is used in math functions.

(F)ootnotes or (E)ndnotes? Notes will be printed either at the end of the page on which they're found or at the end of the file as indicated here.

Section Numbering Style [(R)oman or (N)umeric]? If you choose to automatically number sections, they'll appear in either Roman (I, II, III, A, (b)) or numeric (1, 1.1, 1.1.1, and so on) format. To save the settings and go to the opening page of *MultiMate Advantage II,* press F10.

The opening page contains essentially a blank screen. The cursor indicates where you can begin writing. As soon as the page is onscreen, you can begin typing in your text. In the next chapter, we'll cover details on moving the cursor and text management, but first, let's consider the bit of information that's on the screen.

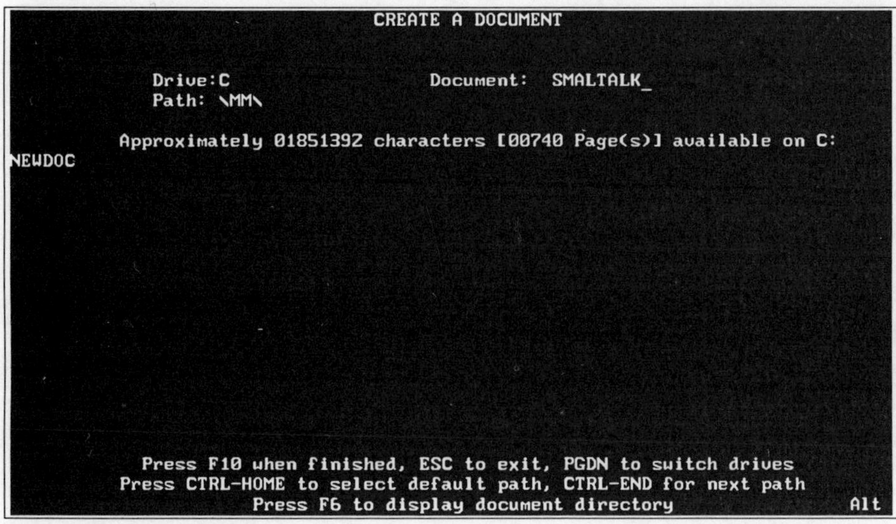

Figure 1-3. Opening Page

Document line. At the very top of your screen should be a line that gives you essential information about the document in which you're working. It will tell you:

Title
Page number
The line number of the cursor
The column number of the cursor

If you're unfamiliar with these terms, try hitting the Enter key a few times. You'll see the cursor move down the screen. You'll also see the line count move, indicating which line you're on. Line 5, for example, is the fifth line down from the top of the current page. Hit the space bar a few times and you'll see the cursor move across the screen. As the cursor moves, the column number in the top line will also move, indicating which character column the cursor is in. The columns are numbered from the left margin. The default setting is 75—the maximum number of characters in the line.

Insert. There's one last heading on the top line that doesn't show up, called *Overwrite*. Overwrite means that any text you type in can be overwritten by new text.

To try this, type in something on the screen (it doesn't matter what you type). Now, use the arrow keys to move the cursor back to the beginning of the line. Now, type in something new. You'll see the new type replace the old. Overwrite is the default setting.

Note: MultiMate Advantage II *has a second type of Insert mode called* Drop Down. *However, most writers prefer to use Insert mode. In Insert mode, new type doesn't replace the old; instead, it "bumps" the old type to the right.*

Push the Ins key on your numeric keypad. You'll see the word INSERT appear on the top line of your screen. Now, move the cursor back to the beginning of the line you just typed, and type a few more words. You'll see the new words inserted in the sentence, "bumping" the old words to the right. You can leave the document in Insert mode as long as you like; however, once you quit the document, the default will reset to Overwrite.

Format Line. Immediately below the Document line is the format line. It tells you how long your line is, where the tabs are set, and how your lines are spaced. (Figure 1-3 shows the format line on an opening page.)

The default format line, indicated by the number 1, shows single spacing, three set tabs, and the end-of-line return symbol («).

Caps Lock and Num Lock. Finally, at the very bottom of the screen on the right-hand side are the letters S and N and arrows.

S: Refers to capital letters. When the arrow points up, you're in Caps Lock mode (all uppercase letters); when it points down, you're in lowercase mode.

N: Refers to Num Lock. When the arrow points up, Num Lock is activated and the numeric keypad types numbers. When the arrow points down, the numeric keypad is for cursor movement.

Saving. Perhaps the most important keys in any word processor are those that save a document to permanent memory. *Multi-Mate Advantage II* utilizes several methods of saving:

- *Save and Exit.* At any time you wish to leave a document, press the F10 key. Your document will automatically be saved and you'll be returned to the main menu.
- *Save and Continue.* If at any time you wish to save text as you're typing, press Shift-F10. The material you've typed will be saved and you'll be returned to the same cursor position in your document.

- *Automatic Saving. MultiMate Advantage II* automatically saves a document every time the cursor moves across a page break. For example, once you type page 1, a page break is automatically inserted and you move to page 2. The material in page 1 is automatically saved, *but not the material on page 2.* You'll need to either save the material on the following page manually or wait until you cross over the next page break for it to save automatically.

Call Up An Existing Document. The procedure is essentially the same for creating a new document. However, instead of typing 2 at the opening menu, type 1.

Hot Start can also be used to call up an existing document. Just be sure you've given the correct path if the document is in a directory other than that of the program.

You now have an overview of starting *MultiMate Advantage II*. In the next chapter we'll discuss basic editing.

Writing Directly to the Printer

MultiMate Advantage II features the ability to use your printer as though it were a typewriter. In this manner, you can quickly type a memo or address an envelope. Here's how it works:

- Make sure your printer is installed properly. If your printer isn't installed for *MultiMate Advantage II,* the function won't work.
- From the main menu, select Additional Print Functions.
- The last two functions from the Additional Print Functions menu are Typewriter Mode (Single Character) and Typewriter Mode (Line).
- Single Character allows you to type one character at a time and send it directly to the printer.
- Line allows you to type out an entire line before sending it to the printer.
- Line is often most useful since you can make corrections to the line that aren't possible with the direct mode of Single Character.

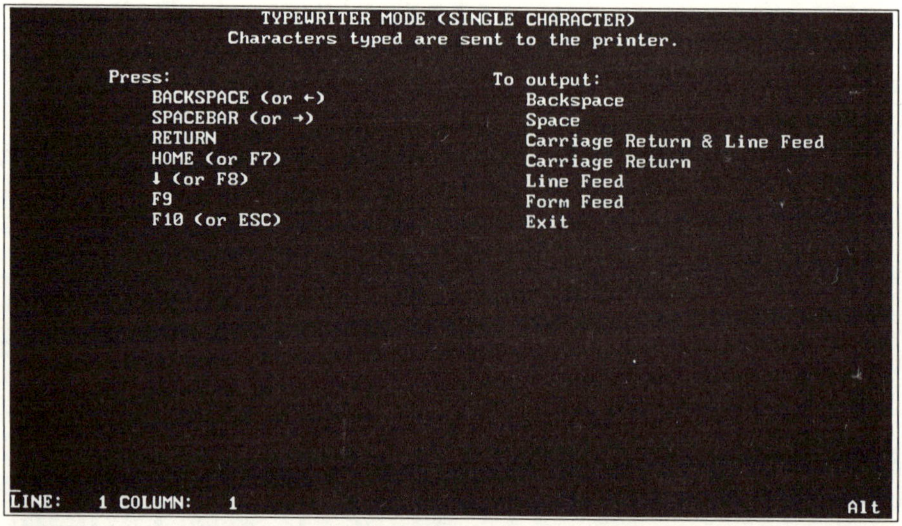

```
                    TYPEWRITER MODE (SINGLE CHARACTER)
                 Characters typed are sent to the printer.

          Press:                              To output:
              BACKSPACE (or ←)                    Backspace
              SPACEBAR (or →)                     Space
              RETURN                              Carriage Return & Line Feed
              HOME (or F7)                        Carriage Return
              ↓ (or F8)                           Line Feed
              F9                                  Form Feed
              F10 (or ESC)                        Exit




















LINE:    1 COLUMN:    1                                                    Alt
```

Figure 1-4. Typewriter Mode (Single Character) Screen

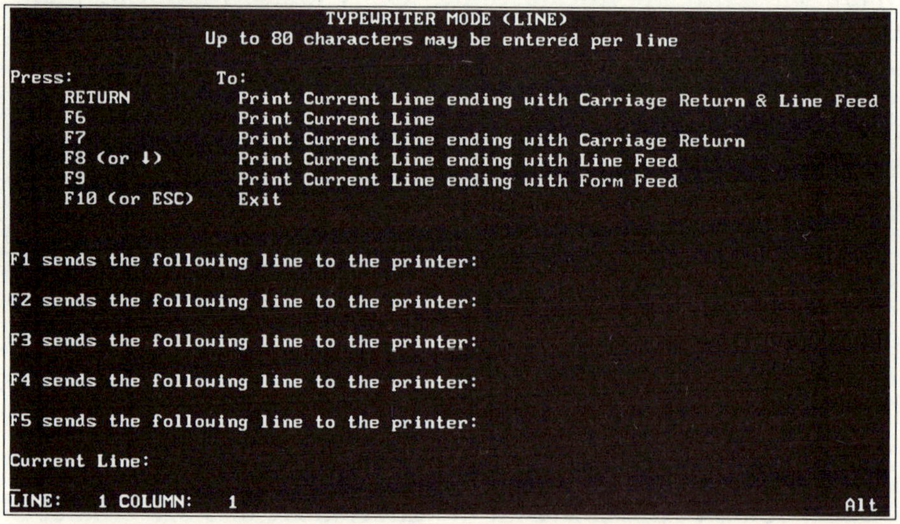

```
                        TYPEWRITER MODE (LINE)
                 Up to 80 characters may be entered per line

Press:              To:
    RETURN              Print Current Line ending with Carriage Return & Line Feed
    F6                  Print Current Line
    F7                  Print Current Line ending with Carriage Return
    F8 (or ↓)           Print Current Line ending with Line Feed
    F9                  Print Current Line ending with Form Feed
    F10 (or ESC)        Exit


F1 sends the following line to the printer:

F2 sends the following line to the printer:

F3 sends the following line to the printer:

F4 sends the following line to the printer:

F5 sends the following line to the printer:

Current Line:
LINE:    1 COLUMN:    1                                                    Alt
```

Figure 1-5. Typewriter Mode (Line) Screen

In Typewriter Mode, you won't be able to use the normal word processing features of *MultiMate Advantage II*. In Line Mode, however, some word processing features are available. These include:

Arrow keys	Move the cursor left or right on the line. Up and down arrow keys do not function.
Backspace	Deletes characters to the left.
Del	Deletes characters to the right. (The minus key may also be used here.)
To enter a line	Press Enter.
To repeat a line	Use the function keys. You may repeat up to five lines. Use F1 for the first line, F2 for the second, F3 for the third, and so forth.

TIP: *MultiMate Advantage II* allows you to enter special printer codes directly from the keypad. You can use the Alt key for this. Enter the codes directly in decimal format. (Check your printer's documentation to see which codes turn different functions on and off.)

With both Character and Line modes, *MultiMate Advantage II* allows you to control some printer functions from the keypad. For example:

To advance the paper	Press F9; the paper will move up one form.
To advance the paper one line	Press F8; in Line Mode, this will print the current line.

Chapter 2
Basic Editing

In this chapter, we'll look at commands you need to know to handle basic letter writing, document editing, graphics, and even manuscript management. As with other chapters in this book, we'll look at the material from the perspective of *function*. If you want to learn about a particular aspect of editing, look for the heading that covers that subject—the corresponding command keys and an explanation of their usage will follow.

Cursor Movement

The *cursor* tells you where you are in a document and moves one character forward each time you type a character or space.

Wordwrap

Since *MultiMate Advantage II* is equipped with automatic wordwrap, there's no need to strike the Enter key at the end of each line. *MultiMate Advantage II* will automatically move the cursor to the beginning of the next line once you reach the maximum number of characters allowed for the line on which you're typing.

Arrow Keys

Arrow keys on the numeric keypad allow you to move the cursor anywhere on the document *except over untyped areas*. To move the cursor into new or blank areas of the document, you must type characters or use the space bar. Holding the arrow keys down will produce repeated rapid movement. Holding the Ctrl key down while pressing either the left or right arrow key will move the cursor to the left or right, respectively, by word instead of by character.

Top of Screen

Press the Home key to go to the first character at the top of the work screen.

Top of Page

Press Ctrl-Home to go to the first character at the top of the current work *page.*

End of Screen

Press End to go to the end of the current screen.

End of Page

Press Ctrl-End to go to the very end of the current work page.

Screen Up or Screen Down

Press PgUp or PgDn to move the screen either up or down by 19 lines. The cursor will remain in the same position.

Previous Page or Next Page

Press Ctrl-PgUp or Ctrl-PgDn to move the screen either to the next page or to the previous page, respectively.

End of Line

Press Alt-F4 to go to the end of a line.

Beginning of Line

Press Alt-F3 to go to the beginning of a line.

Go To Page

To quickly go to any place in the document:
- Press F1.
- Type the number of the page you want to go to.
- Press F10.
- You'll be taken to the top of the requested page.

Beginning of File

Press Home-F1 to go to the beginning of the document.

End of File

Press End-F1 to go to the top of the last page of the document. Then hit Ctrl-End to go to the end of the document.

Cursor Movement Rate

You can vary the cursor movement rate between slow and fast.
On a scale of 0–9, the default is halfway, or 5. The setting can be
changed permanently by accessing the console defaults.

You can change the rate while you're working on a document
by simply pressing the Shift key and using either the minus (−)
or plus (+) keys *on the numeric keypad* to adjust the rate. The
change you make in cursor movement will only be in effect for as
long as you're working on the document. Closing (saving) the file
will reset the cursor rate to the default (5).

*Note: You must use the numeric keypad. Using the regular plus and
minus keys will have no effect.*

Deleting Errors

The real advantage of word processing over regular typewriting is
the ability to correct errors onscreen. *MultiMate Advantage II* provides a series of different methods that allow for making changes
and corrections in a document.

Typeover

MultiMate Advantage II is set in *Overwrite* as its regular mode. This
allows you to move the cursor back over a document, at any
time, and simply type in the correction. The new type will overwrite the old type.

There are two problems with Overwrite:

- First, the new type may not fit where the old type was.
- Second, most experienced word processor users prefer to type
  in the Insert mode, which inserts new type *within* the old, rather than over it.

Both problems are solved by using the Ins Char key to
move *MultiMate Advantage II* into Insert mode.

When you press the Ins Char key, the word INSERT appears in the upper right corner of the screen and allows for the
insertion of new characters in the text. Should you wish to type
over old characters or words at any time, press Ins Char again
(Overwrite mode); INSERT will disappear from the screen.

Delete to the Left

Press the Backspace key to erase characters *to the left* of the
cursor.

Delete to the Right

Press the minus key (−) on the numeric keypad to delete characters to the right of the cursor.

Delete Character Strings

Press Delete to remove a character string, rather than individual characters. (Use the numeric minus [−] key for individual characters.)

To use Delete:

- Place the cursor at the beginning of the string of characters or words you want erased.
- Press the Delete key. At the top right corner of the screen you'll see the words, DELETE WHAT?
- Now move the cursor to the end of the string you want to erase and press Delete again. All the characters in the string will be removed and the text will close in, filling the space.

Highlighting

In order to delete, you must highlight the character string to be deleted. Highlighting is also necessary for many other features of *MultiMate Advantage II,* such as copying or moving text, so it's worth taking the time to learn some *highlighting* tricks provided by the program.

Highlight Using Arrow Keys. The simplest way to highlight is by using the arrow keys. Press Delete to begin highlighting; then press the right arrow key and the highlighting will continue until you release the arrow key. To remove highlighting, use the left arrow key.

Highlight a Screen of Text. Press Page Down to highlight an entire screen of text. To remove the highlighting, use Page Up.

Highlight a Word. Place the cursor on the word to be highlighted. Press Delete (or another highlighting key) and then press Alt-F5. The word will be highlighted.

Highlight a Line. Place the cursor on the line to be highlighted. Press Delete (or another highlighting key) and then press Alt-F6. The line will be highlighted.

Highlight a Sentence. Place the cursor on the sentence to be highlighted. Press Delete (or another highlighting key) and then press Alt-F7. The sentence will be highlighted.

Highlight a Paragraph. Place the cursor on the paragraph to be highlighted. Press Delete (or another highlighting key) and then press Alt-F8. The paragraph will be highlighted.

Undo

What would Delete be without Undo? In publishing, the word *stet,* meaning "leave as originally written," is used to prevent accidental erasures. In *MultiMate Advantage II,* the electronic equivalent of stet is *Undo,* which is executed by pressing the asterisk (*) key.

If you accidentally delete a character, word, or text, you may be able to recall it by using the Undo command. After deleting text or characters with either Delete or the minus key ($-$), you can use the asterisk (*) key on the numeric keypad to undo the previous delete command.

Hold down the asterisk (*) key and the previously deleted text will appear on the screen. When you've exhausted the text temporarily stored in the Undo file, a message will display on the screen stating NO DELETED TEXT TO UNDO.

You may move the cursor before using the Undo command to place deleted text elsewhere in the document if so desired. You may not use the Undo command to restore text removed by using the space bar in Overwrite mode.

Other Commands

So far, we've covered the basic cursor management commands for *MultiMate Advantage II.* There are, however, many other editing commands that are essential for the efficient writer.

Page Breaks

You can insert a page break anywhere in the text of a document. Normally, page breaks are handled automatically, as set up in the opening screens. However, if you want the break to occur at a spot other than the automatic setting (at the end of the number of lines established as the page length), or if you want to create page breaks manually, there are two methods of doing so in *MultiMate Advantage II,* as described below.

Movable Page Break. A movable page break is one that may move if the text is repaginated. Repagination reorganizes the document according to guidelines set in the Document Organization screen (described later); a movable page break acts as a sort of temporary break.

Place the cursor anywhere on the line directly above where you want the page break to occur and press F2. A page break will appear and the format line for the page immediately above it will be brought down.

Immovable Page Break. An immovable page break is one that's tied to the text. This ensures that a break will occur at the designated spot regardless of whether or not the document is repaginated. Place the cursor anywhere on the line immediately above the desired page break and press Alt-B; a new format line will appear with an upside-down *T* symbol, indicating that the page break is immovable.

Removing Page Breaks. Page breaks cannot be removed as such. Instead, the pages before and after the page break can be combined—in effect, removing the break.

Move the cursor to the very end of the page that falls above the page break. Press Shift-F2; the page break will be removed and the above and below pages will be combined.

> **TIP:** It can sometimes be difficult to determine the exact end of a page—since blank spaces are counted, it may be hard to "see" where a page ends. Therefore, it's best to use the Ctrl-End command to take the cursor to the very end of the page before you combine the pages. Memory is limited to 6K when combining pages; if both pages combined have more than 6K of text in them, they can't be combined.

Centering

Any line can be centered simply by using the F3 key. The cursor, however, must be placed before the first character to be centered.

Indenting

There are two methods of indenting, using *MultiMate Advantage II:*

- The first is to simply use the indent key (F4) found in the upper left-hand corner of the standard keypad. This will indent a single line of text to the next tab stop. (Tab stops are indicated on

the format line. See Chapter 3 for information on how to change tab stops.)
* The second method is to create a temporarily indented left margin. Under this method, all lines beginning with the current line will be indented (moved to the next tab stop) until a carriage return is entered.

The indent key is normally used to begin an indented paragraph. Create a temporary margin indent when you want text set off from the left margin.

To establish a temporarily indented left margin:
* Place the cursor at the far left of the line.
* Press F4. A right arrow will appear, moving the line to the right, to the next tab.
* You may continue using F4 to move the left margin over to additional tab marks. Once the tab marks end, the F4 key will move the left margin one line to the right.
* Press Enter to end the indented section.

Repaginate

Repagination is useful when you want to do any of the following:

* Create sections of a document each with a different page length. (One section, for example, could be double spaced and another single spaced.)
* Reformat the pages of a document to make them all the same page length.
* Reorganize the footnotes in a document.

Repagination is achieved by using the Document Reorganization menu, which you can reach by two different methods:

* Press Alt-L to call up the pull-down menus. Highlight "Document Reorganization" on the first menu, which is the Layout menu.
* Pressing Ctrl-F2 will also call up the Document Reorganization menu.

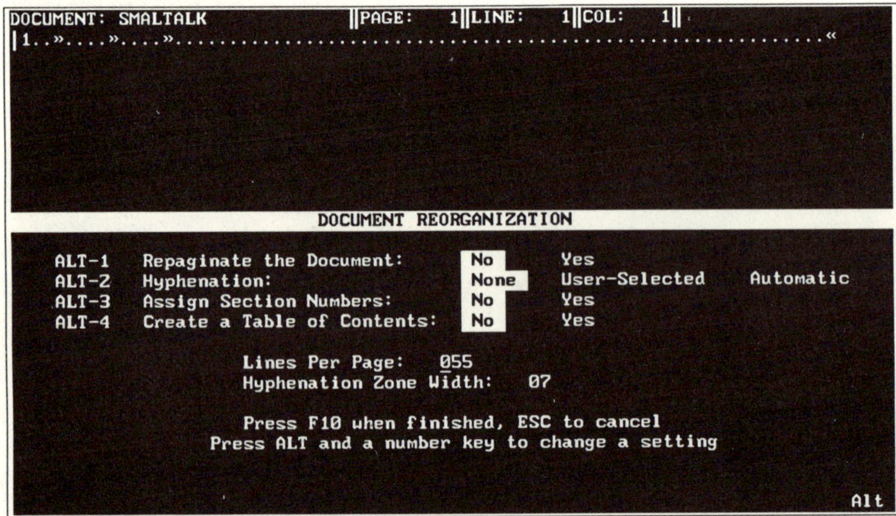

Figure 2-1. Document Reorganization Screen

To repaginate:

- Press ALT-1 to select Repaginate the Document:, the first selection on the Document Reorganization screen.
- Enter the number of lines you want on each page (if the number is different from the original setting in your opening screens).
- Press the F10 key to engage repagination. The document will be repaginated from the point at which the cursor was last placed.
- If you want the entire document repaginated, place the cursor at the beginning of the first page.
- If you want only a section repaginated, place the cursor at the beginning of that section.

(See "Headers and Footers" in Chapter 4.)

Changing the Format

The format line appears at the beginning of the document. It also appears at each page break.

```
DOCUMENT: newdoc                 ‖PAGE:    1‖LINE:    1‖COL:    1‖
|1..»....»....».........................................................«
«
«
«
«
|2..»..................»....»....»....»...»...»......«
    »This format line indicates double spacing and
tabs have been       »added «
    »                 »      »every«
    »                 »      »    »five«
    »                 »      »    »    »columns«
    »                 »      »    »    »    »    »after«
    »column 20




                                                              Alt
```

Figure 2-2. Format Line

The format line tells you the following characteristics of your document:

- Spacing
- Line length
- Tabs

To change the format line:

- Place the cursor under the format line where you wish to change it and press F9. The cursor will immediately move to the format line, allowing you to edit it.

Spacing is given by the number that appears at the far left of the format line. The following spacing is allowed:

0	no spacing
1	single-line
2	double-line
3	triple-line
Q	quarter-line
H	half-line
+	1½-line
=	2½-line

To change the spacing:

• Simply type in a new number, character, or symbol.

Line length is indicated by the return symbol («) at the right of the format line and indicates the maximum length of the line. (To see the maximum line length, move the cursor to the return symbol and check the column number on the document line at the top of your screen.)

To shorten the line:

• Place the cursor on any dot before the return symbol.
• Press Delete. This will shorten the line.

To lengthen the line:

• Press the Insert key.

You may also use the Enter key to set the line parameters:

• Place the cursor at any position on the format line and press Enter. The line length will immediately be set at that position.

To change the tab setting:

• Press the Tab key anywhere on the format line to add a tab.
• Use the Delete key to remove tabs.

To save the new settings:

• Press F9. This also returns the cursor to its previous position, before you adjusted the format line. Format lines can be added anywhere in a document.

Note: The format line does not have to be visible onscreen for it to be adjusted; simply type F9 and the cursor will immediately jump to the previous format line.

To add a new format line:

• Position the cursor at the spot where you want a new format line.
• To repeat the current format line, press Shift-F9.
• To repeat the page format line, press Alt-F9.
• To repeat the system format line, press Ctrl-F9.

The *current format line* is the line immediately above where you're typing. The *page format line* is the line at the top of the page on which you're typing. The *system format line* is the original line that appears at the beginning of the document.

> **TIP:** You can look at a format line at any time without saving it by pressing Esc after any of the above commands. Pressing Esc cancels the command. For example, press Ctrl-F9 and then Esc to look at the system format line without saving it.

Format lines can easily be removed.

To remove a format line:

- Make sure the cursor is below the format line you want to delete.
- Press Delete.
- The words DELETE WHAT? will appear in the upper right-hand corner of your screen.
- Press F9.
- Press Delete again.
- The format line will be removed.

Pull-Down Menus

MultiMate Advantage II offers virtually complete pull-down menus to help the user quickly achieve whatever goal is desired from the programs. The pull-down menus are accessed by pressing Alt-L. These seven menus are shown in Figure 2-3.

Figure 2-3. Pull-Down Menus

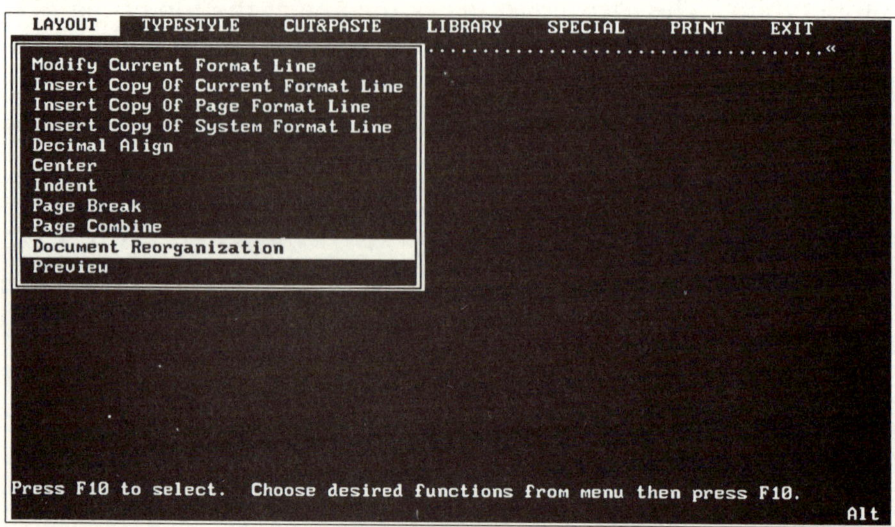

Layout Menu

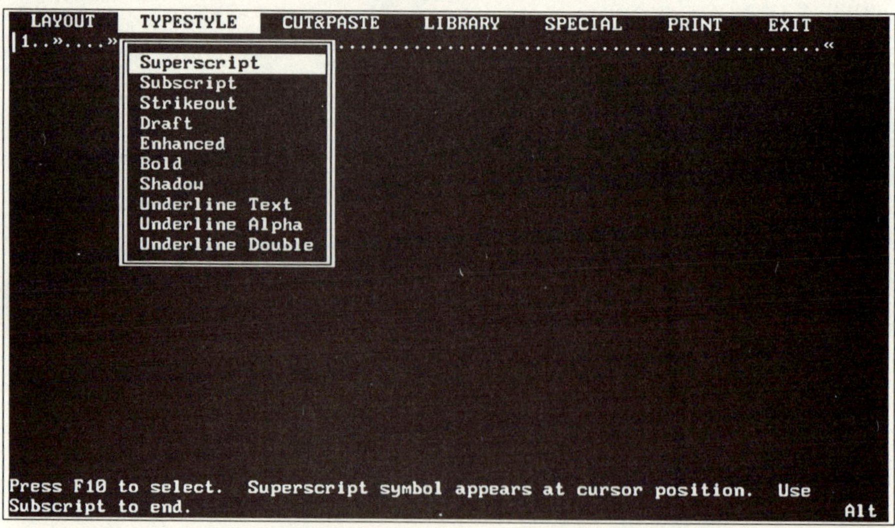

Typestyle Menu

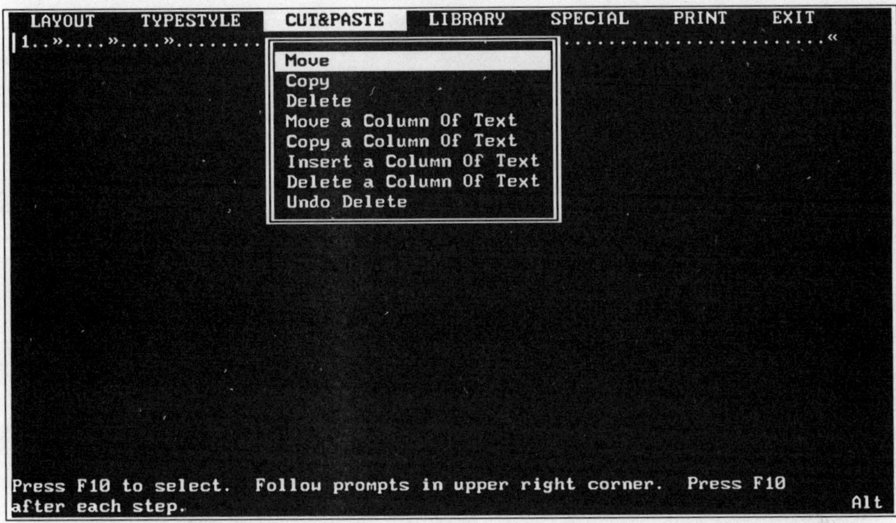

Cut & Paste Menu

Library Menu

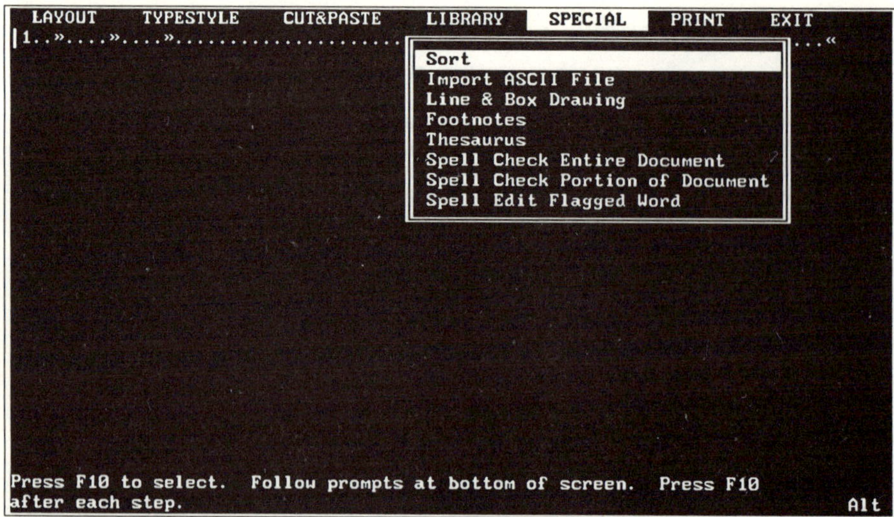

Special Menu

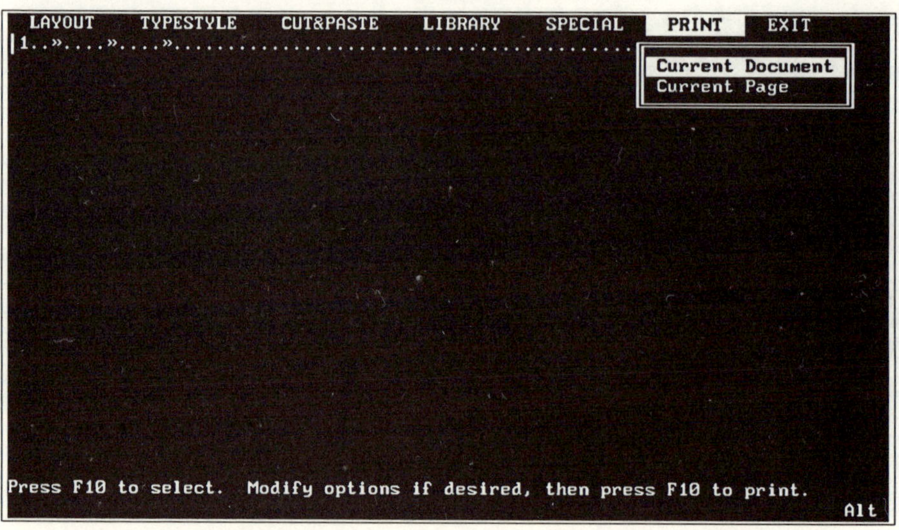

Print Menu

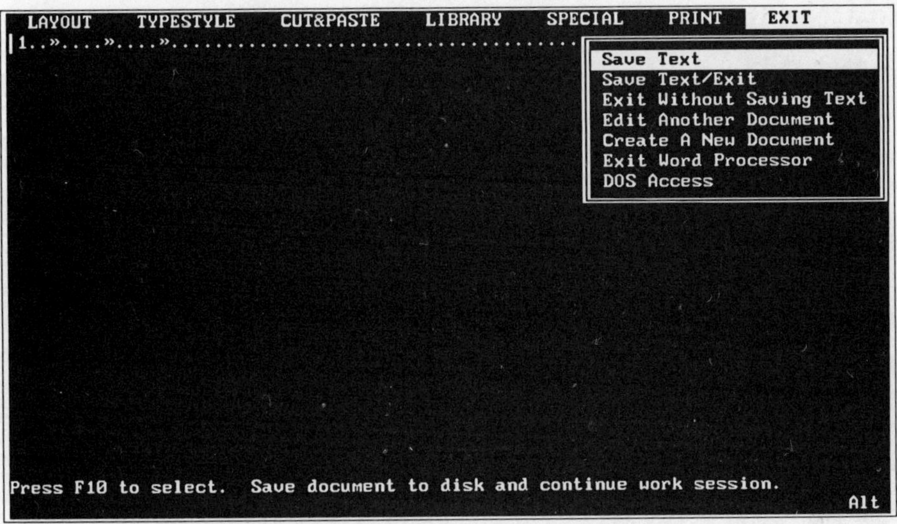

Exit Menu

To select from a pull-down menu:

• Use the up or down arrow keys to highlight your selection.
• Press Enter.

To choose a different menu:

• Use the left and right arrow keys.

To remove menus from the screen:

• Press Esc.

As you move through the pull-down menus, the function described by each command appears at the bottom of the screen. Functions from the pull-down menus will be discussed individually in later chapters.

Graphics

MultiMate Advantage II offers basic graphics from the keypad, allowing you to draw lines of different textures and sizes and to combine these lines to form boxes. *MultiMate Advantage II* does not provide for drawing round lines or circles.

To access the drawing mode from the keypad:

- Press Alt-E.
- A graphics menu will appear at the bottom of your screen, showing six different line options.

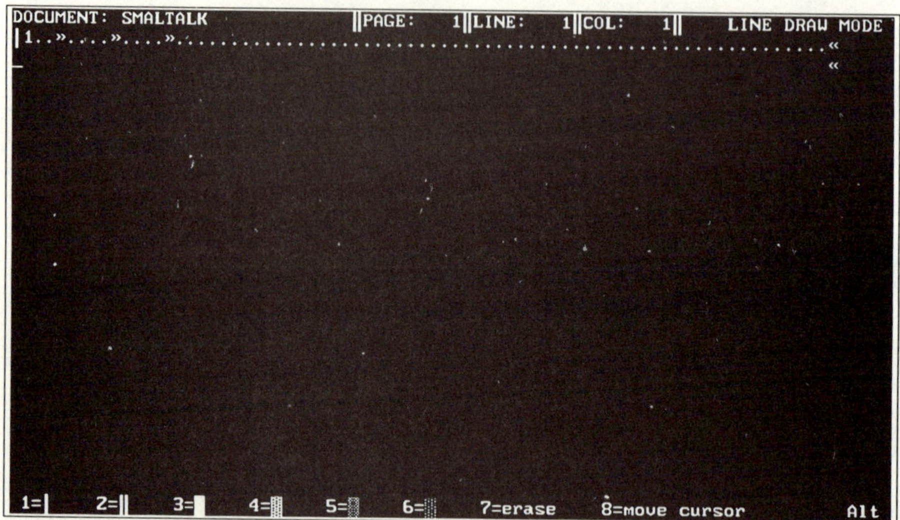

Figure 2-4. Graphics Menu

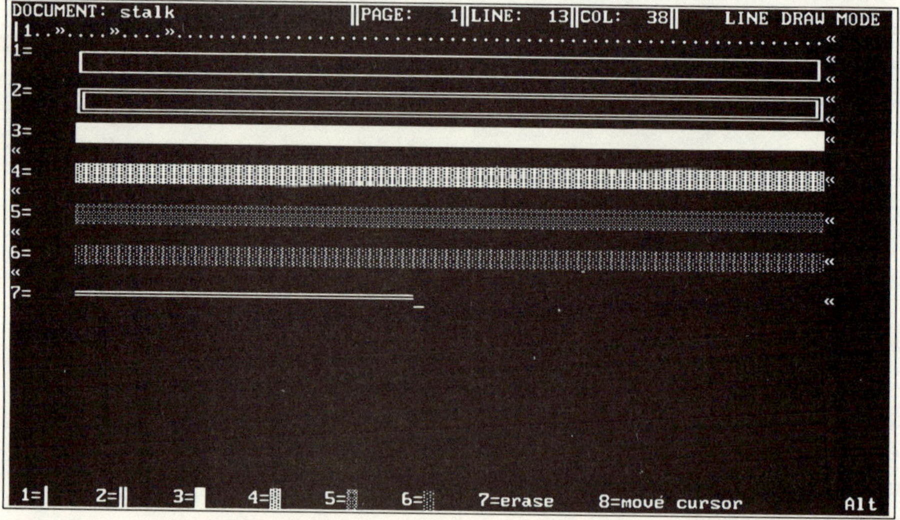

Figure 2-5. Six Line Options

Press the corresponding number key to highlight a selection. Once highlighted, use the arrow keys to draw your selection vertically or horizontally onscreen.

> **TIP:** You can change the form of your line at any point. Simply change the highlighted option on your menu and continue to draw.

To erase existing lines:

• Press 7.

To move the cursor without drawing:

• Press 8.

To save what you've drawn:

• Press F10.

Until you press F10, the lines are only temporary. If you press Esc, the lines will be removed from the screen (if you haven't previously saved them).

Note: After saving your lines, you may erase them with the minus or Del keys.

Drawing Boxes

Select your line format and use the arrow keys to create a box. The box may be as large vertically or horizontally as you choose, and can be used to surround text, if you wish.

Limitations

The line and box drawing functions of *MultiMate Advantage II* will not work completely when you're in either Snake or Bound Column mode. You'll be able to draw lines within a column, but not across column borders.

> **TIP:** You can't draw a line through screen tags, which means you won't be able to draw a line through headers, footers, or format lines. However, you can draw lines around them, and if you use Document Reorganization, your lines should connect when the screen tags disappear at print-out time.

While the line- and box-drawing features of *MultiMate Advantage II* are a welcome addition to the program, they're supported by only a limited number of printers, including the following:

AT & T 473
Brother M-1509
Contronics GLP
C.ITOH ProWriter 24LQ S/SC
C.ITOH 851 ProWriter
C.ITOH 8510 BPI
Cordata (with IBM fonts)
Dataproducts SPG 8051/8052/8071/8072
Diablo 1641/P32CQI/P12CQI
Epson DX35
Epson FX/JX/LX Series (Using EPFXLINE; see Chapter 8)-2
IBM Graphics (80 characters per second speed)
IBM QuietWriter 5201/2
Mannesmann Tally 460/490
NEC 2050 (plug and play)
NEC PinWriter (some models)
Okidata Microline 92/93 (IBM compatible)
Okidata OK 20/192/193/290 (standard)/293 (in IBM mode)
Panasonic KX P1091/1092/1093
Radio Shack DMP 130/420/2100P/2110
Sakata 1200
Sellum
Siemens PT-88
Star Micronics Gemini
Star Micronics Radix 10PC/15PC SG10/SG15
Toshiba P321/P341/PageLaser
Xerox P32CQI
Xerox (Some printers with PC fonts)

Chapter 3

Intermediate Editing

In this chapter, we'll look at some editing chores that tap into the power of *MultiMate Advantage II*. We'll cover tasks you would normally expect to encounter in the course of handling any substantial document.

Copying, Moving, and Deleting Blocks of Text

For copying, moving, and deleting, the procedure is identical. The block of text to be copied, moved, or deleted is first highlighted and then the function (copy, move, or delete) is executed.

Note: Whether your computer can highlight text onscreen is a function of your hardware. Some monitors/computers will not be able to show highlighting. Nevertheless, the copying, moving, or deleting procedures will still work as indicated.

Copying

You may copy a single character, word, line, paragraph, or a larger block of text from any location to any location within a document.

To copy text:

- Determine the part of text you want to copy.
- Place the cursor at the beginning of the text to be copied and press the F8 key.
- The words COPY WHAT? will appear in the upper right-hand corner of your screen.
- Move the cursor to the end of the material to be copied and press the F10 key.
- The words in the upper right-hand corner will change to TO WHERE?
- Place the cursor at the location where you want the material to be copied and press F10 again.
- The text will be copied to that location.

Note: If you want a format line copied along with the text, press F9 after pressing F8, before pressing F10. This will include the current format line in the copy.

Moving

You may move a single character, word, line, paragraph, or a larger block of text from any location to any location within a document.

To move text:

- Determine which part of the text you want to move.
- Place the cursor at the beginning of the text to be moved and press the F7 key.
- The words MOVE WHAT? will appear in the upper right-hand corner of your screen.
- Move the cursor to the end of the material to be moved and press the F10 key.
- The words in the upper right-hand corner will change to TO WHERE?
- Place the cursor at the location you want the text to be moved and press F10 again.
- The text will be moved to the new location.

Note: If you want a format line moved along with the text, press F9 after pressing F8, before pressing F10. This will include the current format line in the move.

Deleting

You may delete a single character, word, line, paragraph, or a larger block of text.

To delete text:

- Determine which part of the text you want to delete.
- Place the cursor at the beginning of the text to be deleted and press the Delete key.
- The words DELETE WHAT? will appear in the upper right-hand corner of your screen.
- Move the cursor to the end of the material to be deleted and press the F10 key.
- The words in the upper right-hand corner will change to TO WHERE?
- Place the cursor at the end of the material to be deleted and press F10 again.
- The text will be deleted.

Margins

MultiMate Advantage II differs from many other word processors in its procedure for setting margins. With *MultiMate,* the final margins for the document are set at print time rather than onscreen.

You can set the *line length* when typing onscreen—the location of the line, as indicated, is determined when you print the document. Line length is set by using the format line (described in Chapter 2) and always begins at the left side of the screen. The length of the line is set by changing the return marker on the line.

To set the line length:

- Place the cursor on the format line by pressing the F9 key.
- Move the cursor to the desired length and press Enter. The new line length is now set.

You can type a document for as long as desired with the new line length. At print-out time, you'll place the text on the page by setting the left margin, using the Document Print Options screen. (A further description of the Document Print Options screen is given in Chapter 8.)

```
Document:  SMTKL3            DOCUMENT PRINT OPTIONS

Start Print At Page Number        001  Left Margin                          000
Stop Print After Page Number      001  Top Margin                           000
Enhanced [N] / Draft [Y]            N  Double Space The Document [N or Y]      N
Number Of Original Copies         001  Default Pitch [4 = 10 CPI]              4

Printer Action Table (PAT)    TTYCRLF  Sheet Feeder Action Table(SAT)
Use:(P)arallel/(S)erial/(F)ile/(L)ist  Sheet Feeder Bin Numbers [0 - 3]
    (A)uxiliary/(C)onsole           P      First Page 0  Middle 0  Last Page 0
Device Number                     001  Char. Width/Translate (CWT)
Pause Between Pages [N or Y]         N  Background / Foreground [B or F]        B

Print Comments [N or Y]             N  Justification [N or Y or (M)icro]      N
Print Doc. Summary Screen [N or Y]  N  Proportional Spacing [N or Y]          N
Print This Screen [N or Y]          N  Lines Per Inch [6 or 8]                6
Header / Footer First Page Number 001  Paper Length (lines per page)        066
Starting Footnote Number[1 - 749] 001  Default Font                           A
                                       Remove Queue Entry When Done [Y or N] Y

Current Time Is     16:25:08           Delay Print Until Time Is    16:25:08
Current Date Is     06/30/1988         Delay Print Until Date Is    06/30/1988

              Press F10 when finished, ESC to exit
           Press F1 for PATs, F2 for SATs, F3 for CWTs            Alt
```

Figure 3-1. Document Print Options Screen

Left and Right Margins

The left margin setting is open to three digits; the number you select will determine its size. Each digit you enter represents one character of type. Since type is measured on the basis of *characters per inch,* you would type in 012 to get a 1-inch left margin for 12-point type; you would type 008 to get a 1-inch left margin for 8-point type; and so on.

The right margin is determined by adding the left margin and the line length. For example, suppose you're using 10-point type and you've already typed in 010 for a 1-inch left margin. Suppose, further, that you're using a 65-character (6½-inch) line length. The right margin equals the left margin plus the line length (1 + 6½), or 7½ inches from the left side of the page. On a standard 8½ × 11 inch page, that makes the right margin 1-inch wide.

Top and Bottom Margins

Top and bottom margins in *MultiMate Advantage II* are set in a similar fashion to the left and right margins. On the Document Print Options screen, you're given the opportunity to set the top margin in *lines.* To translate this into the more conveniently understood inches, enter the number of lines to equal one or more inches.

For example, you're asked onscreen to set the number of lines per page. Suppose you set the number 8. This tells *MultiMate Advantage II* that each inch contains eight lines. For the Top Margin setting, if you now enter the number 008, you're telling *MultiMate Advantage II* that you want a 1-inch top margin. (Remember, you already set eight lines to every inch.) Likewise, if you've established six lines per inch, type 006 for a 1-inch top margin, and so on with other numbers. You can set the top margin to ½ inch, 2 inches, or any height you desire.

The bottom margin is automatically set by adding the top margin and the number of lines per page. For example, if you've set eight lines per inch on the Document Print Option screen, you've selected 008 as the top margin setting (for a 1-inch margin), and you have a document that's 48 lines long (6 inches), your bottom margin will be 4 inches on a standard 11-inch long page. (A 1-inch top margin + 6 inches of text = 7 inches − the 11-inch document length.)

Search and Replace

Any good word processor contains a search-and-replace function. *MultiMate Advantage II* is no exception. *MultiMate Advantage II* allows you to find any character string and then replace it with any other character string. (A character string is any character, word, or group of words.) *MultiMate Advantage II* allows for finding and replacing either in one instance or globally throughout a document.

Search and Replace has a variety of uses in word processing, including the following:

Mnemonics. If you have a difficult or long word or group of words you regularly use, you can simply type in a code. For example, you could use MM to represent *MultiMate Advantage II*, and then, after the document is completed, you could use Search and Replace to remove every occurrence of MM and replace it with *MultiMate Advantage II*. (*MultiMate Advantage II* also provides a *macro* or *key program* that allows you to do this while typing and editing; see Chapter 4.)

Error correction. Perhaps you've written a report in which you use a word or phrase repeatedly, only to discover once you're finished that you used the wrong word or phrase. You can now search for every occurrence of that word or phrase and replace it with the correct one.

Locating. This is especially helpful if you've created a long document. Instead of having to painstakingly search through the document yourself, you can use *MultiMate Advantage II*'s find function to locate the word for you.

Search and Replace is one of the most powerful tools a good word processor offers. Here's how it works in *MultiMate Advantage II*.

Search

The Search command will allow you to find any character string in a document.

To activate the Search menu:

- Place the cursor at the beginning of the document (or at some other point if you don't want to search the entire document) and press the F6 key.

The words SEARCH MODE will appear in the upper right-hand corner of the screen, and the search menu will appear on the lower half of the screen. You're then given two areas—*Case* and *Direction*—in which to make selections.

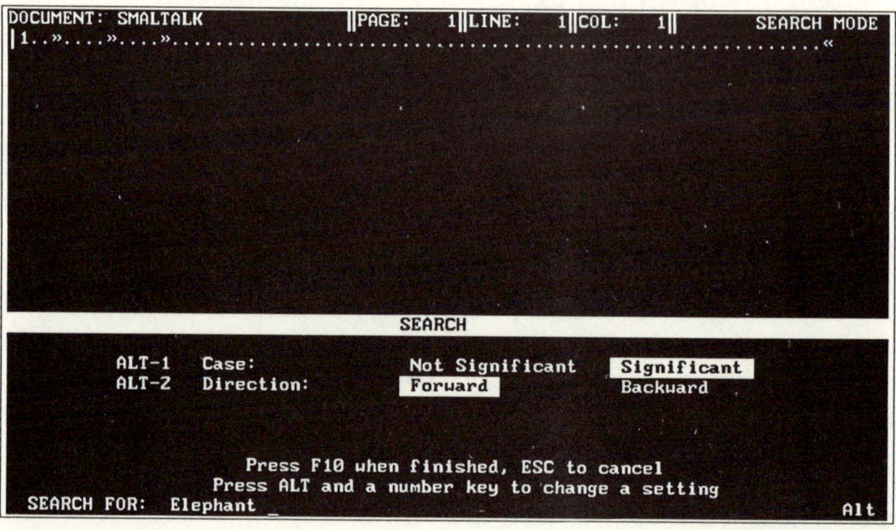

Figure 3-2. Search Menu

Case. You can conduct the search for a string that will match the *case* you've selected. *MultiMate Advantage II* will find only the character string that matches exactly, including both upper- and lowercase letters. For example, if you're looking for "Dynamic" and you select Case: Significant, *MultiMate Advantage II* will ignore "dynamic" and "DYNAMIC." To switch between *Case: Significant* and *Case: Not Significant* (the default setting), press Alt-1.

Direction. Choose either *Forward* or *Backward* for the search, which will depend upon you're location in the file and in which direction you believe the character string is located. Forward is the default setting.

At the bottom of the screen, the words SEARCH FOR: indicate where to type the character string you want to find. The maximum length of a string is 49 characters, including spaces. Type a space before and after your character string if you don't want the program to search for occurrences *within* other words.

To activate the Search function:

- Press the F10 key.
- *MultiMate Advantage II* will search through the document until it matches the character string you've typed; it will then move the cursor to that place in the document.

To repeat the procedure:

- Press the F6 key again.
- *MultiMate Advantage II* will search and find the next occurrence of that string each time you press the F6 key.
- When the entire document has been searched and no remaining matches are found, the program will signal NO MATCH FOUND.

To end the search:

- Press Esc.

Search and Replace

MultiMate Advantage II will allow you not only to search for a character string, but also to replace it with another character string. The procedure is similar to Search.

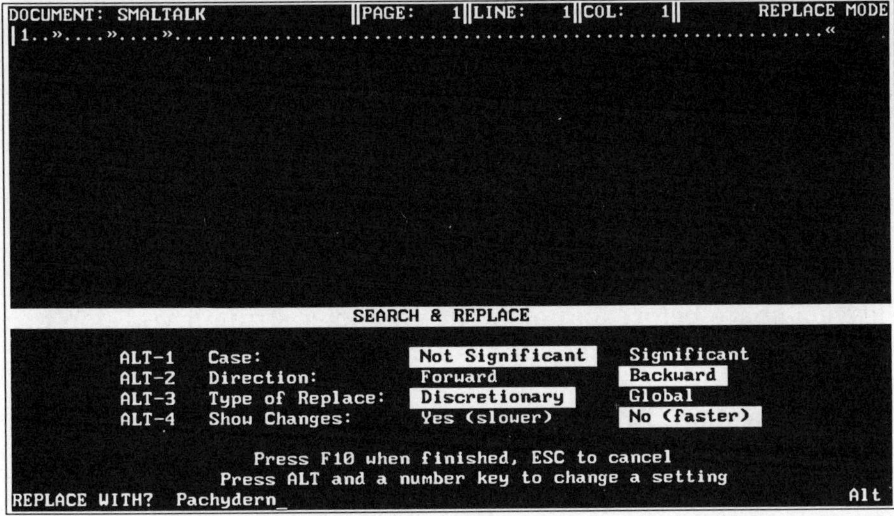

Figure 3-3. Search and Replace Menu

To activate the Search and Replace menu:

• Press Shift-F6.

The first two items on the Search and Replace menu are identical to those on the Search menu. You're asked whether you want to match the case and whether to search forward or backward. The third and fourth items are *Type and Replace:* and *Show Changes:*.

Type and Replace:. This asks you how you want the search conducted. If you choose *Discretionary,* the program will stop at every occurrence of the selected character string and give you the option of making the replacement. The words REPLACE? Y\N\ANY OTHER KEY TO CANCEL will appear onscreen. If you want the old string or character replaced with the new, press the Y key. If you don't want it replaced, press the N key.

In either case, *MultiMate Advantage II* will move on to the next occurrence. Cancel the search by pressing any other key. *Global* tells the program to make the replacements itself. It will automatically replace the new character string with the old without asking for your approval. To choose between Discretionary and Global, press Alt-F3.

Show Changes:. If you selected Global, you can decide whether to have the changes echoed to the screen as they're made. If you choose *No* to Show Changes:, the program will move along much faster. To choose *Yes* to see the changes made press Alt-4.

To activate Search and Replace:

• When the Search and Replace menu is activated, the words REPLACE WHAT? appear at the bottom of the screen.
• Type in the character string (up to 49 characters, including spaces) you want replaced, and press Shift-F6. (Remember to leave a space before and after the character string if you don't want *MultiMate Advantage II* to find occurrences of it within other words.)
• A new question, REPLACE WITH? will appear.
• Enter the new string you want replaced and press F10. *MultiMate Advantage II* will search through your document and make the replacements as indicated.

To end Search and Replace anywhere in the document:

• Press Esc.

Format Lines: Search or Replace

MultiMate Advantage II can also find and/or replace format lines. The procedure is similar to that for normal searching, but when you're asked what to search for, press the F9 key. The program will look through the document, calling up the various format lines.

To replace a format line:

• First decide whether you want a Discretionary or Global replacement. (Unless you've used the same type of format lines throughout the document, select Discretionary. This allows you to decide whether to replace a given line.)
• Press F9. (Press Control-F9 for the system format line; press Alt-F9 for the page format line.)
• Modify the format line once it appears onscreen.
• Press the F10 key. If you selected Global, the program will search and replace all occurrences of the format line. If you selected Discretionary, the program will stop at each occurrence and ask whether you want the line replaced before moving onto the next occurrence.

To end Search and Replace at any time:

• Press the Esc key.

Note: All programs as complex as MultiMate Advantage II are likely to have a few bugs. In some versions, pressing the Esc key will cause the program to lock up. If this happens, there's nothing you can do except try a warm boot. (Although Ashton-Tate says this shouldn't happen, it has happened on my version and on another.)

If the program locks up, you'll lose everything typed in your document back to the last save. In some cases, when the file is reopened, you may even find some saved material that's imperiled, as MultiMate Advantage II may not be able to fully recover the file.

If this should occur, DO NOT ENTER ANY MORE INFORMATION INTO YOUR FILE. Close the file by pressing Esc and selecting Y for DO YOU WISH TO ESCAPE WITHOUT SAVING THIS PAGE? Then use the Document Recovery function found on the Utilities main menu to recover as much of the file as possible.

Chapter 4
Advanced Editing

In this chapter, we'll consider several different editing techniques that are both useful and sophisticated. While the title of this chapter is "Advanced Editing," there is nothing esoteric or even complex about these techniques. Even the complete beginner can pick them up after a few instructions. What's advanced about these techniques is the way they *function* within the word processor. In this chapter, we'll cover columns, macros, footnotes, and formats.

Columns

MultiMate Advantage II allows you to create up to eight columns on a page. You can vary both the width and length of columns. In addition, you can link the columns together so the text at the bottom of the first column continues at the top of the next on the same page (called *snaking;* phone books typically use this format); or, you can keep the columns separate so the text in each column is independent (or *bound*). This type of column is useful for writing scripts.

Creating Bound Columns

MultiMate Advantage II uses the term *bound* to describe independent columns of text. Scripts, for example, use bound columns, with text in one column and comments in another, separate column. Bound columns are easy to create; their basic structure is determined by the format line. Columns can be created anywhere on a format line simply by including brackets ([ ]).

```
DOCUMENT: SMALTALK                    ‖PAGE:    1‖LINE:   13‖COL:   41‖
│1-[------------------]----[----------------------------]-----------------«------
     The above format line     ◄
     creates two columns
     of unequal lengths.
     Simply adding the
     brackets creates the
     columns. Spaces left
     between the brackets
     indicate the width
     between columns.◄
           ◄                   ◄
           ◄                   ◄
           ◄                   THE TEXT IN EACH COLUMN IS
                               INDEPENDENT_



                                                                          Alt
```

Figure 4-1. Bound Columns Showing Brackets in the Format Line

The only trick to creating bound columns is adding the text. In Column Mode, the cursor will automatically move to the top line of the first column.

To edit a bound column:

• Press Shift-F3. You may now enter as much text as desired.

If you go over the number of lines set for a page, a page break will automatically be inserted (if Automatic Page Break is turned on). The text will continue in another column until you instruct *MultiMate Advantage II* to end it.

To insert a hard break into the text:

• Press Shift-F3 and then hit Enter. This inserts a hard column break "◄" into the text; the cursor automatically moves up to the beginning of the next column.

You can enter separate information into as many different columns as desired.

Snake Columns

In addition to bound columns, *MultiMate Advantage II* provides for *snake* columns in which information "flows" from one column to the next, in the same manner as listings in a telephone book. Text continues from the bottom of the first column, to the top of the second column, into the third column, and so on.

Snake columns, unlike bound columns, must be of equal width—both left and right justified—and are generated automatically by *MultiMate Advantage II*.

To create a snake column:

- Create a new format line just above the point at which you want to begin Column Mode, or access an existing format line.
  Press Shift-F9 to get to the *current format* line.
  Press Alt-F9 to get to the *page format* line.
  Press Ctrl-F9 to get to the *system format* line.
- Once the cursor is on the format line, follow a procedure similar to that of creating a bound column: Use the bracket keys ([ ]) to indicate the width of the first column you want to create.
- After using the brackets to indicate the width of the column and its location on the page, indicate how many columns you would like by typing in the number. You may select up to *eight columns.*

Figure 4-2 shows how a three-column format line would look and the way the resulting columns would appear.

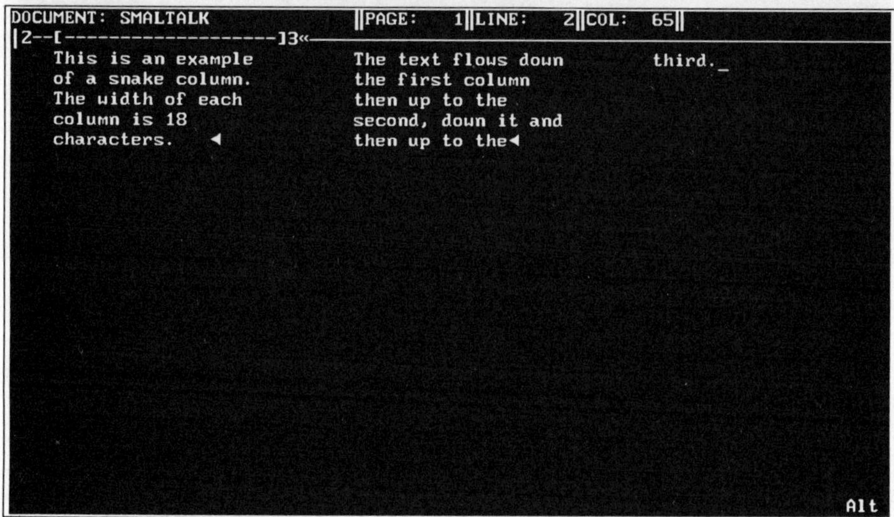

Figure 4-2. Snake Column

Determining snake column lengths

Column length is determined by two different factors—the amount of text you have to enter and the Page break (if you've installed automatic page breaks.)

Long columns. For long snake columns, simply set up the columns and begin typing in text. If you've opted for automatic page breaks, the text will jump to the beginning of the next column when you reach the end of the page. (If you want the text to continue in the original column, set the Automatic Page Break to *off.*)

Short columns. If you're going to have a rather small amount of text in your columns, a different method is easier to use. After setting up the column format line, go to the *first column* and type in *all* the text you want to reformat into short columns.

When you're finished typing in the text, switch to Column Mode and press Shift-F3 and then Ctrl-F2. The text will jump into snake format.

Making long columns short. Sometimes it's necessary to change a long-column format to short columns—for example, if you planned on a full three-column page, only to find yourself short of text after typing it all in (Figure 4-3), you would need to switch to short columns.

Figure 4-3. Long Snake Column

You now need a method of "balancing" the columns. This is quickly accomplished by again shifting into Column Mode and pressing Shift-F3 and then Ctrl-F2. The columns will immediately "balance."

Column Groups

MultiMate Advantage II recognizes that you may want more than just a single set of bound columns; you may want several *groups,* or horizontal sections, of columns. Figure 4-4 features an example of a column group.

```
DOCUMENT: SMALTALK              ||PAGE:    1||LINE:   2||COL:   33||        INSERT
|2-[-------------------]----[-------------------]----[-------------------]«
    «                        3 COLUMNS◄             TEXT IN EACH IS
    «                                               INDEPENDENT OF THE
    The text in this                                OTHER◄
    example has been
    entered into 3
    columns.◄
    ◄                        ANOTHER 3 COLUMNS◄        ◄
    In addition a            ◄                       TEXT IS STILL
    separate column                                  INDEPENDENT IN EACH
    group has been                                   OF THE COLUMNS.◄
    created.◄




                                                                          Alt
```

Figure 4-4. Column Group Within Three Bound Columns

Column groups are created by using Ctrl-Enter, which places a diamond-shaped symbol (♦) at the end of the last column to indicate that the group has been completed. Remember, you can always shift into and out of Column Mode by using Shift-F3.

When editing in Column Mode, the cursor may not behave as you anticipate because the basic cursor movements are slightly adjusted to allow for the columns. The difference is that instead of sending the cursor anywhere on the screen, the cursor controls will send the cursor anywhere you direct *within a column.* Thus, using the left cursor arrow may only send the cursor to the left margin of a column, *not into the adjoining left column.* To get to the next column you may have to use the down arrow key to send the cursor to the end of that column and then up to the top of the next.

Nevertheless, adjusting to Column Mode is usually quite easy. Also, *MultiMate Advantage II* includes a number of functions for additional flexibility that involve the use of the F3 key (in Column Mode) as follows.

To go to the beginning of the column:
• Shift-F3-Home

To go to the end of the column:
• Shift-F3-End

To go to the next column group:
• Shift-F3–Up Arrow

To return to the previous column group:
• Shift-F3–Down Arrow

To return to the previous column:
• Shift-F3–Left Arrow

To advance to the next column:
• Shift-F3–Right Arrow

Just as with bound columns, it's possible to create horizontal groups of snaked columns. Simply tell *MultiMate Advantage II* where the first column ends.

To end a column group:
• Press Ctrl-Enter.

To end one column and move to the top of the next:
• Press Ctrl-Enter.

Creating Tabular Columns

When you're working with phone numbers instead of text, or you want to create columns of figures that can be added, subtracted, or otherwise dealt with using *MultiMate Advantage II*'s mathematical functions (Chapter 9), you need a *tabular* column. Text tabular columns are created by adding tabs to the format line. You can have as many tabular columns as desired, keeping in mind that text moves across the page rather than down. Figure 4-5 shows a typical tabular column.

```
DOCUMENT: SMALTALK              ║PAGE:    1║LINE:    1║COL:    1║
│1----»-----------------»-----------------»-----------------«----
«
«
1      »John James       »1121 Milford Avenue»Miles Landing«
2      »Sally Matthews   »324 Siesta          »Longsville«
3      »Albert Smith     »1309 Ressol Rd.     »Sawtooth Landing«




                                                          Alt
```

Figure 4-5. Tabular Column

To create a tab column:

- Create a new format line or move to an existing format line (see the preceding instructions).
- Use the space bar to remove any existing tab markers.
- Use the Tab key to insert new tab settings (the procedure is very much like setting the tabs on a typewriter).
- Press the F9 or F10 key to return to the text. You can now use the Tab key to tab over to each setting as you type.

Macros (Key Procedures)

A *macro* (or what *MultiMate Advantage II* calls *key procedure*) is a type of recording: It records a series of keystrokes on your keypad and plays them back at your designation.

Although macros are most frequently found in spreadsheets, where they're used to recreate formulas or series of entries, they can have very useful functions in word processors as well. For example, a macro can be very convenient and time-saving when used to call up a frequently used series of words or paragraphs. Throughout this book, I use the words *MultiMate Advantage II*, but rather than type in the words at every occurrence, I made use of a macro to help me out. I typed the words *MultiMate Advantage II* into a "key" file (which recorded each keystroke as it was executed) identified by the letters MM. Then, whenever I needed to type in those words, I simply called up the key file utility and typed MM. The program did the rest, writing out the words onscreen.

With *MultiMate Advantage II*'s macro system, you can record virtually any keystroke possible, creating a very large file or a very small file, whichever suits your purposes—and you can play it back in any document.

Limitations of Macros

At first glance, the macro seems like an excellent way to create a "boilerplate" for a document. Perhaps you're in real estate and you constantly prepare leases—you have a series of clauses you want inserted in some leases and not in others. One way of handling this would be to store each clause in a separate key. The problem is that it takes time for *MultiMate Advantage II* to type out an entire clause; so, for longer documents, a macro isn't the best method if it doesn't save you time. To create a longer "boilerplate," a better solution would be to merge a short file into your document. Instructions for merging documents are in Chapter 7.

Creating a Macro

While macros can be created in almost every area of *MultiMate Advantage II* (the exceptions are Help and Print Queue), you'll almost always use them exclusively within a document. When you're in a document and you want to create a macro, use the following procedure.

Place the cursor at the point where you want to begin recording the macro. (A macro cannot record data that was previously typed—you must retype it for the macro.)

To invoke a macro:

• Press Ctrl-F5.

You'll be prompted to give the macro a name and a directory location. Be sure the name you give doesn't correspond to any other macro file names or the new file will erase the old. In naming macros, the rule is *the shorter the better*. Opt for letters that quickly remind you of what the macro contains—for example, the letters MM to call up *MultiMate Advantage II*. After naming the macro, proceed as follows.

To begin recording a macro:

• Press the F10 key.

WARNING: From this point forward, every keystroke will be recorded and played back. Take care not to make careless entries. In addition to numerals and letters, all other keys are recorded, including the movement keys (such as the arrow keys), Enter, Delete, and function keys.

For example, if you type and then backspace to and type out the corrected version, every keystroke will be recorded. When the macro is played back, it will first type out the word in its misspelled form, backspace as you did, and then finally type out the corrected form.

To end recording:

• Press Ctrl-F5. The recording will end.

Note: To know you're in record mode, check the reverse image "B" at the bottom of the screen, which appears only when the program is in Record Mode.

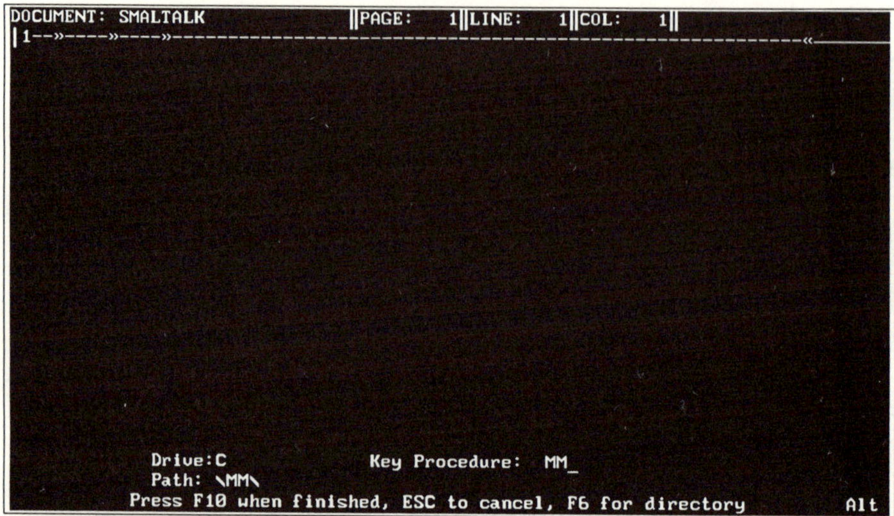

Figure 4-6. File Menu (Macro ID Box)

Playing Back a Macro

You can play back a macro at any point in a document. The procedure is simple.

To play back a macro:

- Place the cursor where you want the macro to begin.
- Press Ctrl-F8. The macro ID box will appear onscreen.
- Identify the key name you've given your macro as well as the directory to which it refers.
- Press F10. The macro will immediately begin playing back onscreen at about the same rate as your originally typed-in keystrokes.

To pause a macro:

- Press Ctrl–Num Lock.

To restart a macro:

- Press Enter.

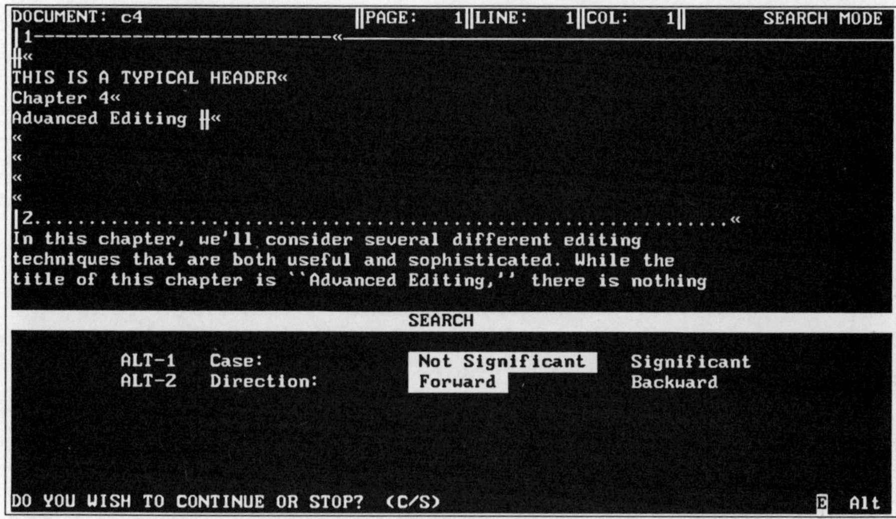

Figure 4-7. Inserting a Pause Within a Macro

Advanced Macro Features

MultiMate Advantage II offers some advanced macro features you
may wish to use, or, you may find these too esoteric for your
needs. It's suggested, however, that you at least read through
them before deciding their amount of utility for you.

Inserting a Pause

One of the more useful functions of a macro is with an address,
phone number, or other changing text, in which you need to type
in information not contained in the macro. For example, as a
business application, you may create a macro that writes out your
letterhead and then asks you for the date and correspondent, and
then continues with the standard billing information.

In order to achieve this, you must insert a pause when you
create the macro at the point where you want to be able to insert
text during playback.

To create a pause:

- Press Ctrl-F7. *MultiMate Advantage II* will notify you that it has
  accepted the command by briefly flashing the word PROMPT
  onscreen. When you play back the macro, at the prompt point

where you inserted the pause, the macro will stop and display these words: PRESS (C) TO CONTINUE. PLEASE ENTER DATA, THEN CTRL-F6 TO RESUME.
• Enter the data.
• Press Ctrl-F6 to continue with your macro.

Customizing Your Macro

It's possible to create a customized prompt from within your macro, not only to pause the macro, but also to suggest what should appear where. The following is an example.

Ctrl-F5

INVOICE‹q#›

ENTER NAME OF CLIENT HERE:

— .Ctrl-F6
.Ctrl-F6 should appear ON the line in the position shown.

In the above macro, begin the procedure (presumably naming the macro and continuing on) by writing out the name of a report and then typing in the words, ENTER NAME OF CLIENT HERE:.
Presumably, you wouldn't want these words to appear in the final invoice. You can avoid this by using the up arrow key to move the cursor back to where you wrote ENTER NAME OF CLIENT HERE: and then delete it. When the macro is played back, it will pause and tell you where to enter the name. After you enter the name, it will restart, go back, and erase the prompt.
Beware when customizing macros—they're *thoughtless* programs and will execute exactly what you type in, even if it means typing over text that's already onscreen. You must be careful to place lines and type keys exactly where you want them.

To pause the playback of a Macro:

• Press Ctrl-F7 to get the prompt DO YOU WISH TO CONTINUE OR STOP (C/S).
• Press C or S for *Continue* or *Stop*.

Editing Macros

Editing a macro is complex and time-consuming because macros are written in program rather than document form. The easiest way to edit a short macro is to simply start over and record a new one. For longer macros, *MultiMate Advantage II* provides an editing utility.

To edit a macro:

* Exit any document you're working on and enter the Utilities File section of *MultiMate Advantage II*.
* When you're in the Utilities menu, select Key Procedure Edit, which will take you to the editing section for macros.

The first screen you're shown will ask you to identify the macro you wish to edit. Be sure to give the directory and subdirectory if you're using a hard disk drive.

Figure 4-8. Typical Macro in Editing Form

Unlike using a word processor to write, using a macro editor requires several steps to accomplish each change. The macro editor is divided into three modes: *Cursor Mode, Delete Mode,* and *Insert Mode*.

Each mode accomplishes a different function, and all are self-explanatory. When in Cursor Mode, you can move the cursor across the screen, using the arrow keys. When you're in Delete Mode, you can delete keypresses from the macro. When you're in Insert Mode, you can insert keypresses.

The only complex thing to remember is that you must continually switch modes in order to change functions or locations within the macro.

For example, to correct the spelling of the word *cohice*, you must use Cursor Mode to place the cursor over the letter *o;* then exit Cursor Mode and use Delete Mode to delete the letters *oh;* and finally, exit Delete Mode and enter Insert mode to add the letters *ho,* changing the word to *choice*.

Working within a word processor, you would expect to have all these modes ready instantly; within the macro editor, however, you must physically shift modes in order to accomplish different functions.

To exit a mode:

• Press Ctrl-M.

To move between modes:

• Use the arrow keys.

To select a mode:

• Press the F10 key.

To exit the program:

• Select Exit or use the Esc key to move back through the menus of the Utilities File.

Footnotes

MultiMate Advantage II contains an excellent system for the creation of footnotes. Because of the way the program is designed, footnotes always remain close to the referenced text and print out automatically at the bottom of the appropriate page.

To create a footnote while typing a document:

• Place the cursor *immediately following* the text to be footnoted.
• Type Alt-V[1].

Your screen will change and the Footnote Screen will appear, which is essentially the same as the Document Screen. It contains a format line that can be edited in the same way as the format line in the Document Screen. You may enter as much text as you like in the footnote, up to one page. You may edit the footnote just as you would edit any other text. All editing keys function normally in this mode.

To quit a footnote without saving it:

- Press Esc to cancel the footnote at anytime before saving it.
- You'll be prompted, DO YOU WISH TO ESCAPE WITHOUT SAVING THIS FOOTNOTE? (Y/N); simply answer appropriately.

To save a footnote:

- Press the F10 key.

Your footnote will be saved in a separate file. A musical note (♪) will indicate the location of your footnote. (The appearance of the note will depend on the quality of your monitor.)

Note: Footnotes will not appear in place onscreen; rather, they'll be merged with your document at the bottom of the referenced page during printout.

To edit a footnote after saving:

- Place the cursor directly on top of the musical note (♪).
- Press Alt-V. The document you're writing will disappear and the footnote will reappear.

> **TIP:** You may create as many footnotes as you like. However, the same musical note (♪) will appear for each footnote. Remember, the footnotes are printed out, but do not appear onscreen.

To number a footnote:

- Place the number (#) symbol in the footnote where you want it to appear.
- When the footnote is printed out, the number will automatically be added.
- If you have more than one footnote, include the number symbol in each; they'll be numbered automatically, in order of appearance, in the text.

To delete a footnote:

- Simply remove the musical note (♪) in your document for the footnote you want deleted.
- Do this either by typing over the musical note (when in Overtype Mode) or by placing the cursor on the note and using the minus (−) key.

Repaginating with a Footnote

It's important to repaginate the document after you've added your footnotes. Repagination counts the number of lines on a page and leaves room for the footnote at the bottom of the page for which referenced text occurs.

To repaginate after using Footnote:

- Press Alt-L.
- Select LAYOUT/DOCUMENT REORGANIZATION to quickly repaginate.

Headers and Footers

Headers and *footers* are pieces of textual information appearing on the printout at the top and/or bottom, respectively, of each page. Typically, they contain chapter titles, page numbers, date and time, and so forth. Headers and footers, which are repeated throughout each page of a document, should *not* be confused with footnotes that are tied to specific text.

MultiMate Advantage II allows for separate headers and footers for bound-style documents. A bound document is one with left- and right-hand pages. You can have the same header on both left and right pages, or have one header on the left, and a different header on the right. *MultiMate Advantage II* also allows for the importation of the time/date/hour/filename automatically in the header and footer.

Finally, headers and footers can be tied to pages, or they can be tied to text. If a header is tied to a page, it's included with the text in the number of lines per page. If it's tied to the text, it isn't counted with the lines of text.

Creating a Header

To create a header:

- Place the cursor on the first column of the first line of the first page of your document.
- Press Alt-H (for *header*). A small cross symbol (⊞) appears at the left-hand margin. DO NOT WRITE ANYTHING FURTHER ON THIS LINE.
- Press Enter, which will move you down one line.
- Now type whatever you want in the header. You may write up to five lines of header information.
- Press Alt-H and a second cross (⊞) will appear.
- Whatever you've written will now appear on *every* page of your document.

```
DOCUMENT: c4                        ‖PAGE:   1‖LINE:   7‖COL:   1‖          INSERT
|1----------------------------«
⊞«
THIS IS A TYPICAL HEADER«
Chapter 4«
Advanced Editing ⊞«
«
«
«
|2...........................................................«
In this chapter, we'll consider several different editing
techniques that are both useful and sophisticated. While the
title of this chapter is ``Advanced Editing,'' there is nothing
esoteric or even complex about these techniques. Even the
complete beginner can pick them up after a few instructions.
What's advanced about these techniques is the way they function
within the word processor. In this chapter, we'll cover columns,
macros, footnotes, and formats.  «
«
«
Columns «
«
MultiMate Advantage II allows you to create up to eight columns
on a page. You can vary both the width and length of columns.  In
                                                                        Alt
```

Figure 4-9. Header

You can create a different header to appear on alternating pages of your document.

To separate right and left page headers:

- Go to the very top of the *second* page of your document and repeat the procedure (just outlined) for creating a header.
- Whatever you write will be printed as a header on all *even-num-*

bered pages of the document. Whatever you wrote on page 1 will appear on all *odd-numbered* pages of the document.

You can change a header at any time. The new header will appear and be repeated throughout the remainder of the document. You can also create different secondary left and right headers.

To change a header:

• Simply type a new header on the first page on which you want the change to appear.

Remove a header by creating a "blank header." Simply follow the procedure outlined for creating a regular header, but instead of entering text, enter only a *carriage return* to create the "empty header." The blank header will cancel out any previous headers.

To create a blank header:

• Press Alt-H
• Press Enter
• Press Alt-H
• Press Enter

Creating a Footer

Footers operate almost exactly like headers.

To create a footer:

• Move the cursor to the very first column of the last line of the document.
• Press Alt-F (for *footer*).
• A small *f* appears at the left of the screen.
• Type in the line number on which you want the footer to appear. For example, if you want the footer to appear on line 25 (double-spaced) of each page, type 25, and press Enter.
• Enter your textual material.

To return to text mode:

• Press Enter.
• Press Alt-F once again.
• Press Enter.

```
DOCUMENT: c4              ║PAGE:   1║LINE:  44║COL:   2║          INSERT
f50«
THIS IS A TYPICAL FOOTER«
GETTING THE MOST OUT OF MULTIMATE ADVANTAGE II - PAGE &PAGE&«
f«
|2..».....».....».........................................«
«
link the columns together so the text at the bottom of
the first column continues at the top of the next on
the same page (called snaking; phone books typically
use this format); or, you can keep the columns
separate so that the text in each column is
independent (or bound). This type of column is useful
for writing scripts.«
«
Creating Bound Columns «
«
MultiMate Advantage II uses the term bound to describe
independent columns of text.  Scripts, for example,
use bound columns, with text in one column and
comments in another, separate column. Bound columns
are easy to create; their basic structure is
determined by the format line. Columns can be created
anywhere on a format line simply by including
                                                            Alt
```

Figure 4-10. Footer

You can create a different footer to appear on alternating pages of your document.

To separate right and left page footers:

- Go to the very top of the *second* page of your document and repeat the procedure just outlined for creating a footer.
- Whatever you write will be printed as a footer on all *even-numbered* pages of the document. Whatever you wrote on page 1 will appear on all *odd-numbered* pages of the document.

You can change a footer at any time. The new footer will appear and be repeated throughout the remainder of the document. You can also create different secondary left and right footers.

To change a footer:

- Simply type a new footer on the first page on which you want the change to appear.

Remove a footer by creating a "blank footer." Follow the procedure outlined for creating a regular footer, but instead of entering text, enter only a *carriage return* to create an "empty footer." The blank footer will cancel out any previous footers.

To create a blank footer:

- Press Alt-F.
- Press Enter.
- Press Alt-F.
- Press Enter.

Page Numbers

You can enter a document page number in the footer simply by adding a pound sign (#). The page number will automatically print out.

Date/Time/Page/Document Title

You can automatically print a number of items in either a header or a footer by using the following commands:

&page&	Prints the current page number.
&time&	Prints the time from the operating system.
&date&	Prints the date from the operating system.

Note: The preceding commands will work only if you've previously entered the correct date and time into your operating system or if your hardware enters it automatically.

&doc&	Prints the file document title.
&page&	Prints the last page number.

Text or Page Associated

You must tell *MultiMate Advantage II* whether you want your headers and footers to be *text* or *page associated* (the default is page associated). The command is given on the Modify Document Defaults menu when you open the document.

Page associated headers and footers are included in the line count on each page. In addition, they remain where you placed them.

Text associated headers and footers are *not* included in the line count on each page. Headers become page breaks and remain with the original text in which they were entered.

Chapter 5

Document Management

At various times it becomes necessary to perform large-scale management operations on a document. This means we want to perform one or more of the following changes:

- Copy
- Move
- Delete
- Rename

These can all be handled directly by the DOS operating system. However, if you aren't overly familiar with DOS commands or you don't want to fully exit the program, you can perform these operations totally within *MultiMate Advantage II*.

To save a file while exiting from within a document:

- Press F10. You're now back at the opening menu.

To get to the Document Management menu:

- Type 6. You'll immediately be taken to a new menu that will give you management options.

The first four selections on this menu give basic Document Management operations, which we'll cover one at a time.

Copy a Document

This allows you to copy a document from one disk or subdirectory to another. You're given the option of choosing any document on any drive or directory to send to any drive or directory.

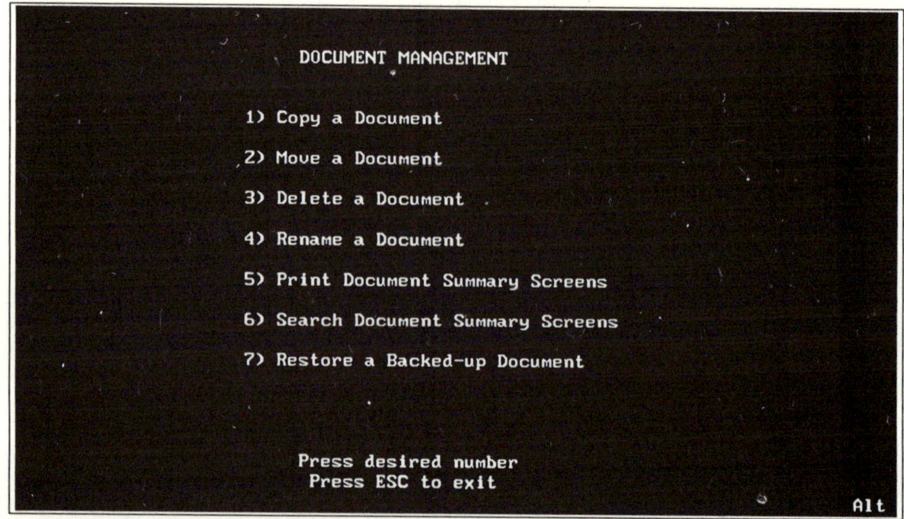

Figure 5-1. Document Management Menu

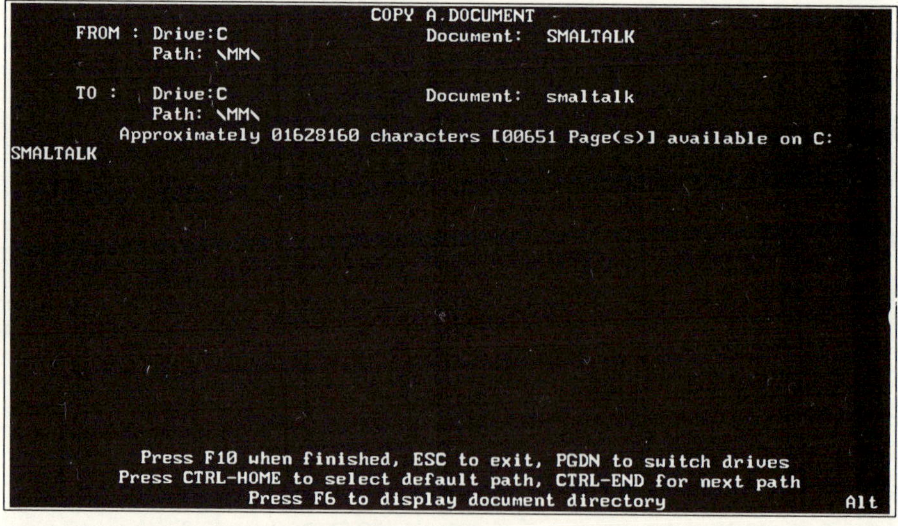

Figure 5-2. Copy Selection Box

To copy a document:

- Engage Copy a Document from the Document Management menu.
- Fill in the *exact* name of the file you want copied, including any extension.
- Press the F10 key. Be sure you have the drive/directories entered correctly.

TIP: You may change the name of the document in the copying process. Simply assign a different name to the document in the TO box.

Move a Document

The procedure for moving a document is essentially the same for copying with one exception: After the document is copied to its new location, *MultiMate Advantage II* deletes it from its original location.

To move a document:

- Engage Move a Document from the management menu.
- Fill in the *exact* name of the file you want moved, including any extension.
- Press the F10 key. Carefully indicate the drive/directories for the move.

Delete a Document

This powerful command should be used sparingly—once you delete a file, you cannot recover it through *MultiMate Advantage II*.

Note: A deleted file can be recovered, in some cases, through the use of special document management programs such as Norton Utilities. *If you've made a backup of the file (discussed in the following section), it can be renamed the same name as the original file. Usually, most of the document can be saved.*

To delete a document:

- Engage Delete a Document from the management menu.
- Indicate the filename, disk drive, and directory.
- Press the F10 key. *MultiMate Advantage II* will delete the file.

Rename a Document

You can give a file any new name that uses the standard eight-characters-plus-extension DOS naming system.

To rename a document:

- Engage Rename a Document from the management menu. The menu called up is the same as that for the copying and moving functions.
- Type in the old filename where *MultiMate Advantage II* asks FROM:, and give the disk drive and path, if any.
- Insert the new name, disk drive, and path where the program asks, TO:.
- Press F10. The name of the file will be changed.

Creating a Document Backup

If you're familiar with computers, you know that in a word processor, the data goes into the computer's random access (RAM), or temporary, memory and is echoed onto the screen for you to see. As long as the text remains in RAM, it's volatile, which means if you turn off the computer or there's a power interruption, whatever you've written thus far will be lost.

To avoid this potentially disastrous consequence, *MultiMate Advantage II* automatically saves a document each time it passes a page break or when the file is closed. This is called *backing up* the file.

Creating a second file before editing is another kind of backing up, and is also important for word processor users. In the process of editing, you can change a document significantly, so it's necessary to have a backup of the original.

To create a backup file before editing:

- The Modify Document screen appears whenever a file is opened. At the setting, BACKUP BEFORE EDITING, the default is *No*.
- Change the default setting to *Yes*.

Now, whenever you open the document, *MultiMate Advantage II* will automatically create a copy of the document with the same filename and extension *.dbk*.

Footnotes and Tables of Contents can be backed up as well;

footnotes use an *.fnb* extension while tables of contents use *.tcb*. In effect, *MultiMate Advantage II* creates a whole new file for you—a copy of the original that will remain available no matter how much you edit the original.

CAUTION: Since MultiMate Advantage II *creates a backup each time you reopen your file, the "original" will change each time to the most recently edited file.*

Saving the Original

You have two options if you want to permanently save your original document:

• The first option is to copy the original document and give it a different name (using the Copy function). For example, if your file is titled "LETTER," you could call the copy file "LETTER1." Now you have two files—one to save permanently and the other to edit.

   If you've engaged the backup function, you'll still get an automatic backup each time you edit the file.

• The second option is to change the filename of your backup file, using either the Rename function or handling it through DOS. When using this option, it's important to leave the .dbk extension on the file and to change only the main filename. Leaving the .dbk extension allows you to restore the file at a later date.

Restoring a Backed-Up Document

To restore a backed-up document:

• Engage Restore a Backed-Up Document from the Document Management menu (item 6 on the main menu).
• Give the full directory and subdirectory paths when you're asked for the document location.
• If you're unsure of the document name, once you've listed the directory location, press F6 to get a list of available documents.
• Enter the name of the document to be restored.
• Press F10 (or press Esc to cancel).

   MultiMate Advantage II will now restore the document to its original form.

Note: The edited version of your file will be destroyed in the restoration process. If you want to save the edited version, use the Rename (or Copy) function to create a separate file.

Removing a Backup File

To prevent accidental erasures, *MultiMate Advantage II* doesn't allow users to remove backup files. You can, however, clear backup files from your permanent memory by using the DOS command ERASE or DEL from the DOS prompt—for example, C:ERASE LETTER1.

Be sure you're in the correct directory for the file when you give the command, or that you list the full path as part of the command—for example, C:ERASE C:\DATA\LETTERS\LETTER1.

Chapter 6

Spell Check, Custom Dictionary, and Thesaurus

MultiMate Advantage II includes a sophisticated spell checker that allows you to run through a file quickly to see which words are misspelled; then, you select from a list of suggested corrections or type in your own correction. You can even add unusual words to one of several "Custom Dictionaries" you create, and search for synonyms of words in the *MultiMate Advantage II* Thesaurus.

The Spell Checker

Some users don't take advantage of *MultiMate Advantage II*'s spell checker because they're unfamiliar with it or hesitant about taking the time to learn it. This is unfortunate because *MultiMate Advantage II*'s Spell Check function is quick to learn, easy to use, and very effective.

Spell Checking from Within a Document

If you're in a document you've just finished writing and you want to check for misspelled words, you can engage *MultiMate Advantage II*'s Spell Check function right where you are, from within the document.

To use Spell Check from within a document:

- Place the cursor at the very beginning of the document.
- Press Ctrl-F10. This engages *MultiMate Advantage II*'s Spell Check function. Note that the character below the cursor is now highlighted.
- Highlight the entire document, or the area of the document you want checked. (*MultiMate Advantage II*'s spell checker looks only at highlighted areas of the document.)
  To highlight the document:
  Press the F1 key, which activates Go To.

Press End, which takes you to the last page of the document.

Press Ctrl-End, which takes you to the very end of the
document.

• Press F10.

MultiMate Advantage II will now spell check the entire document. Two registers will appear at the bottom of your screen: The
first will record the number of misspelled words; the second will
record the total number of words checked.

*Note: The total number of words checked isn't necessarily the total
number of words in the document: MultiMate Advantage II counts all
character strings as words, even strings such as II or F3.*

When the spell checker completes the document, you're returned to the beginning of it (where you started) and the number
of spelling errors is given. From that point, you simply make the
corrections using Spell Edit.

To engage the Spell Edit function:

• Press Alt-F10. This engages the editing portion of the spell
checker.

You're now ready to proceed. *MultiMate Advantage II* indicates each suspect character string by making it blink. The spelling editor will move the cursor to each of these instances, one by
one, where you'll have the opportunity to make corrections.

```
DOCUMENT: c6                          ║PAGE:   1║LINE:  52║COL:   33║
even add an unusual word to a custom dictionary.«
    Unfortunately, some users seldom take advantage of the
spelling checker simply because they are unfamiliar with it
and are hesitant to take the time to learn.  That's unfortunate
since the program is quick to learn, easy to use and very
effective.«

|2---»----»---»------------------------------------------------«________
«
GETTING THE MOST FROM MULTIMATE ADVANTAGE II - Page 1«
«
«
«
«
«

                    Please enter desired function
        0)     Add this word to the Custom Dictionary
        1)     Ignore this place mark and find the next mark
        2)     Clear this place mark and find the next mark
        3)     List possible correct spellings
        4)     Type replacement spelling
        5)     Delete a word from the Custom Dictionary
        ESC)   End Spell Edit and resume Document Edit
                                                              Alt
```

Figure 6-1. Spell Edit Screen

When *MultiMate Advantage II* encounters the first suspected error, you're given an editing screen from which to make a selection (Figure 6-1).

To correct spelling errors:

• Make your selection from the Spell Edit menu. *MultiMate Advantage II* will quickly move from marked word to marked word, and in a few moments, you'll have checked your entire document for spelling.
• When the program is finished checking, it will indicate that it finds no more errors.
• Press any key to exit Spell Check.

This procedure should handle 90 percent of most users' spell-checking needs. For the other 10 percent, a closer examination of the program is required.

Spell Checking a Portion of a Document

You can spell check a page, paragraph, sentence, or word from within the document.

To spell check a portion of a document:

• Place the cursor at the beginning of the area you want checked.
• Press Ctrl-F10 to engage the spell checker.
• Highlight only the portion of text you want spell checked.

To highlight a portion of text, use either the arrow keys or one of the following:

Alt-F5 Highlights the *word* on which the cursor is placed.
Alt-F6 Highlights the *line* on which the cursor is placed.
Alt-F7 Highlights the *sentence* in which the cursor is placed.
Alt-F8 Highlights the *paragraph* in which the cursor is placed.
End   Highlights all text to the end of the screen.

• Once the appropriate text is highlighted, press F10 to engage the Spell Check function.

Spell Checking from Outside a Document

You don't have to be inside a document to use the Spell Check function.

To spell check a document without opening it:

- Select 8 from the main menu.
- Give the full filename, path, and directory for the document you wish to check.
- After entering the correct information, press F10. *MultiMate Advantage II* will ask you which pages you want checked.

> *To spell check the entire document:*
>   Press F10 again.
> *To spell check only selected pages:*
>   Indicate the page numbers and press F10. The appropriate pages will be checked.

The Custom Dictionary

MultiMate Advantage II uses a full-size dictionary to compare your spelling of every word during Spell Check and marks a word when it finds a spelling that doesn't match that of the dictionary.

Unfortunately, although *MultiMate Advantage II* is a highly sophisticated program, it isn't a *thinking* machine, so there are many word usages the program will highlight as errors that are actually correct. For example, the program will often mark names of individuals, unusual abbreviations, and technical words, even though they're correct. Although you can tell *MultiMate Advantage II* to ignore these during Spell Edit, it's a nuisance to have to do so on a one-by-one basis when the words keep popping up.

To avoid this, the program includes a special custom dictionary. You can add your own special words, names, abbreviations, or technical terms to the dictionary. Once added, *MultiMate Advantage II* will check the standard dictionary as well as your custom dictionary for matches. If it finds a match in either, it will ignore the word so you won't have to repeatedly tell the program to ignore the same word.

To add a word to your custom dictionary:

- When you're in Spell Edit and you come across a special word, press the 0 key.

This will tell *MultiMate Advantage II* that you want to add the word to your custom dictionary. (The program may also ask if the word should be capitalized or if it must have a certain piece of punctuation.)

To delete a word from your custom dictionary:

• Press the 5 key.

TIP: *MultiMate Advantage II* only looks for exact matches. Thus, if you add the word *Advantage* to your custom dictionary, the program may still ask you about instances of the following words:

Advantages
Advantaged
ADVANTAGE

You'll have to enter each usage of a word into your custom dictionary, or the program will mark it during the spelling check.

Suggested Replacement Words

If you press the F3 key while editing in Spell Check, *MultiMate Advantage II* will give you a list of possible correct spellings for the word—possibly as many as nine spellings. When looking for a correct version of a word, *MultiMate Advantage II* tries to find words spelled similarly to the one you've written. When the program presents you with a correct spelling in its list of possible spellings, select the number that corresponds with the word. The old word will be replaced with the selected word.

When *MultiMate Advantage II* is unsuccessful with its versions of spellings, you'll need to spell out the word yourself. Select number 4, which allows you to type in the replacement word. (If desired, you can later rerun Spell Check to be sure your replacement word is spelled correctly throughout the document.)

Editing the Custom Dictionary

MultiMate Advantage II uses the *Merriam-Webster Dictionary* to correct spelling. The dictionary is contained in several files labeled WEBSTER, WEBAUX, and WEBSYN.

When you call up the spell checker or the Thesaurus, your words are compared to correctly spelled words contained in the dictionary files. Of course, as noted before, you can create your own custom dictionary. The purpose is to add proper nouns, such as names, and technical words significant to your purposes.

You may want to create several specialized dictionaries. For example, you could use one dictionary when you're writing and editing technical materials, another for letters, and yet another for mailings lists. The number of dictionary uses is endless. Having several different dictionaries speeds up *MultiMate Advantage II*'s spell checking since it only has to check one small dictionary of specialized words, rather than one very large customized dictionary.

To edit the custom dictionary:

• Exit the word processor and return to the main menu.
• Select Custom Dictionary Utility from the main menu.

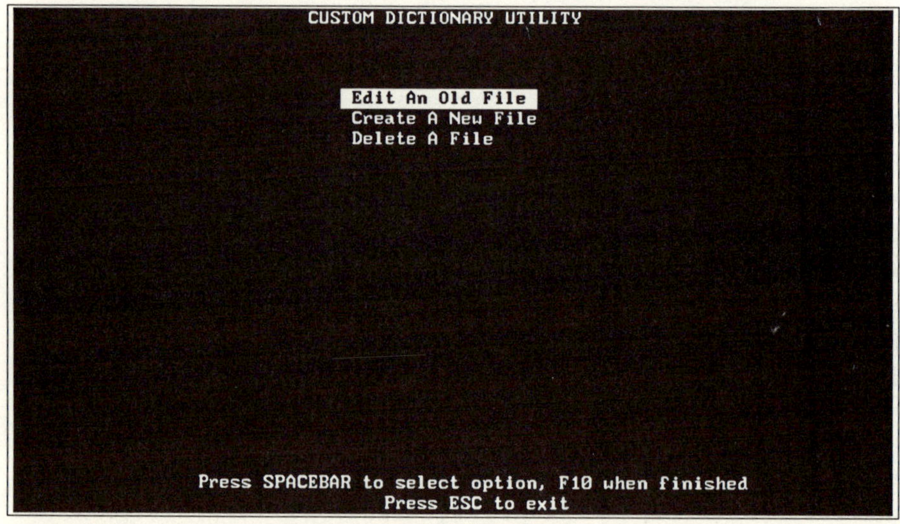

Figure 6-2. Custom Dictionary Utility Screen

The Custom Dictionary Utility offers you three options: Edit An Old File, Create A New File, and Delete A File.

Edit an Old File

You're immediately given a choice of which dictionary you want to edit.

Note: You can't edit the Merriam-Webster dictionaries, only the cus-

tom dictionaries. If you have only one custom dictionary, it will be named CLAMFL, the default.

Figure 6-3. Edit an Old File Screen

Select a dictionary. As soon as you select a dictionary to edit, a new screen will give you two more options: *Modify Custom Dictionary* and *Reorganize Custom Dictionary*.

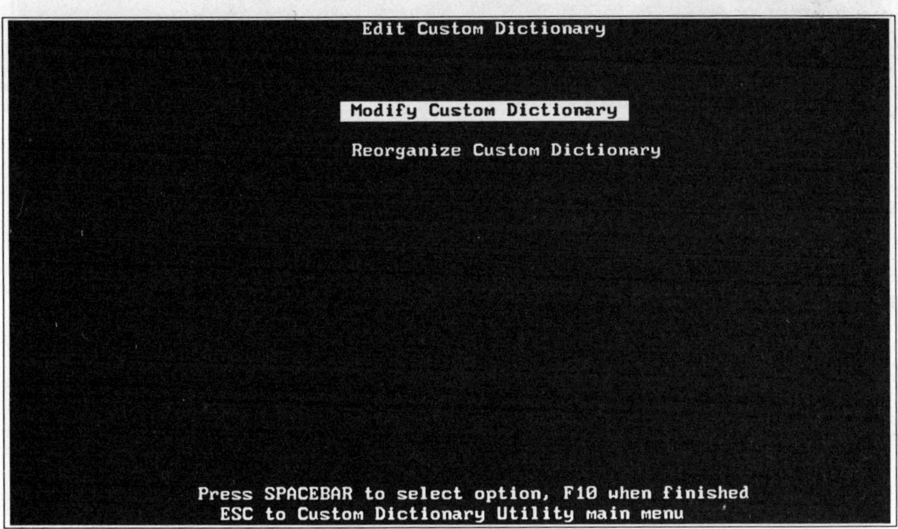

Figure 6-4. Edit Custom Dictionary Screen

Reorganizing the custom dictionary allows you to reorganize the dictionary, making *MultiMate Advantage II*'s access to the words in the dictionary much easier during the Spell Check and Spell Edit functions. The procedure for reorganizing a custom dictionary is virtually automatic. Simply follow the instructions onscreen.

Modifying the custom dictionary allows you to add or delete words.

To add a word(s) to the Custom Dictionary:

- Select Add Word from the Modify Custom Dictionary Screen. A new screen will appear.
- Type in the word(s) you want to add. Press Enter after each word if you enter more than one word.
- Press F10 when you're finished typing in all the words you want to add.

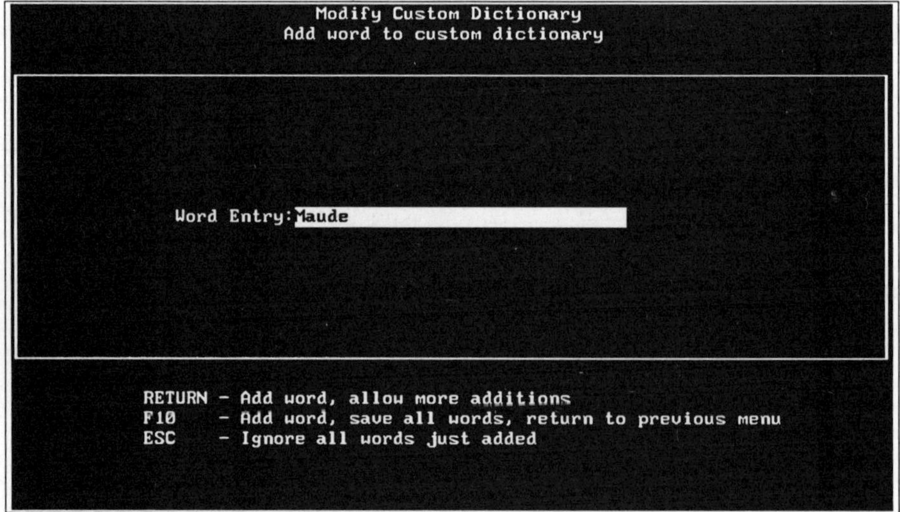

Figure 6-5. Add Word to Custom Dictionary Screen

To delete a word:

- Select View/Delete form the Modify Custom Dictionary Screen. *MultiMate Advantage II* will display all words from the custom dictionary.
- Highlight the word and press Del to remove it.

• To save your changes, press F10.
  To leave without saving your changes, press Esc.

Create A New File

To Create a Custom Dictionary:

• Select Create A New File from the Custom Dictionary Utility.
  All existing directories will be displayed onscreen.
• Type in the name of the new dictionary and the full path and
  directory.

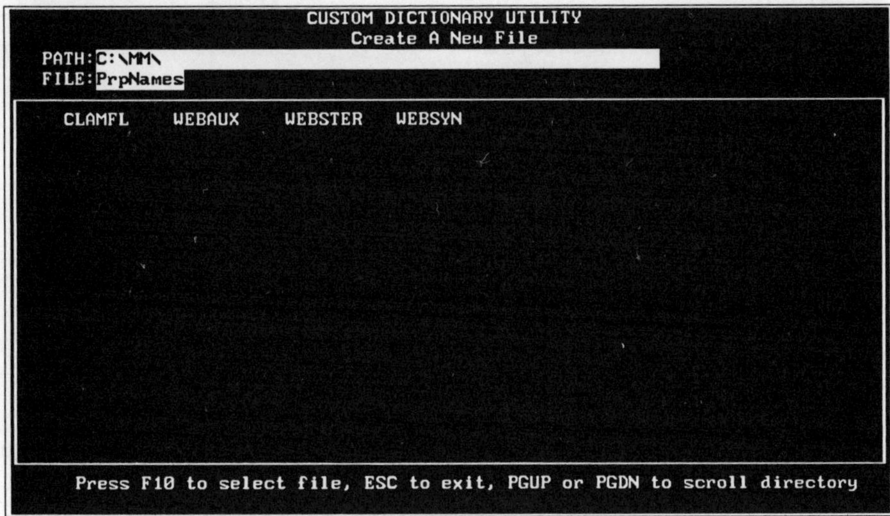

Figure 6-6. Create a New File

TIP: Place the new dictionary in the same subdirectory as your
other dictionaries, or you may have a hard time finding it
when you want to use it.

Delete A File

To delete a Custom Dictionary file:

• Select Delete A File from the Custom Dictionary Utility. All existing directories will be displayed onscreen.

- Highlight the dictionary you want to delete.
- Press F10. The dictionary will be deleted.

TIP: Be careful not to delete a dictionary until you've checked inside to be sure you won't be using those words again. It's usually better to delete *individual words* from a dictionary rather than delete the entire file.

The Thesaurus

It's often the case, when inside a document, that you've not only spelled a word incorrectly, you've also used the wrong word. You may look at the word, scratch your head, and say to yourself, "That's not right." But what is right?

MultiMate Advantage II can help with its online Thesaurus. You can ask the program to check the word (or even a phrase) in question for synonyms. During the check, the program will also tell you the part of speech the word represents as well as its definition.

To call up the Thesaurus:

- Place the cursor on the word or phrase in question.
- Press Alt-T (for *Thesaurus*).
- The Thesaurus will highlight the suspect word. In addition, LOOK UP WHAT? appears in the top right of your screen.
- Press F10 and the Thesaurus will go to work for you.

TIP: You may adjust the highlighting to include more than one word—for example, a phrase. However, unless the phrase is common, the program won't be able to offer much help. In such a case, you're better off just asking the Thesaurus for a single word.

```
DOCUMENT: c6                        ║PAGE:    1║LINE:  53║COL:  60║
    Unfortunately, some users seldom take advantage of the
spelling checker simply because they are unfamiliar with it and
are hesitant to take the time to learn.  That's unfortunate
since the program is quick to learn, easy to use and very
effective.«

|2---»----»----»-------------------------------«________________
«
GETTING THE MOST FROM MULTIMATE ADVANTAGE II - Page 1«
«
«
                           THESAURUS
                         unfortunate

    adj:  of a kind to cause great distress


1) deplorable           4) dire              7) grievous
2) afflictive           5) distressing       8) heartbreaking
3) calamitous           6) dolorous          9) lamentable


Enter Number for Replacement,  ESC - Exit Thesaurus,  ALT-T - Look Up New Word.
SPACEBAR for More Synonyms  PGDN - Next Meaning      PGUP - Prior Meaning.      Alt
```

Figure 6·7. Thesaurus Screen

If your word is acknowledged, you'll be told what part of speech the word represents and its meaning, and you'll be given a list of possible synonyms.

To select a synonym:

• Press the number in front of the synonym.

Note: The number of choices you have will vary depending on the word—some will have many choices, others will have few.

Using the Thesaurus to Best Advantage

The Thesaurus is actually a suggestion machine: It doesn't tell you what you can substitute, it merely offers suggestions. To get the most use from the Thesaurus, you need to see as many suggestions from the program as possible. Be sure you see all possible synonyms for the suspect word. Some words have more than one meaning, in which case you can use the PgUp and PgDn keys to scroll through the other available meanings and synonyms.

Since the Thesaurus can list only nine synonyms onscreen, you should check for additional ones. If there are more, the program will note this in the section containing the directions at the bottom of the screen. You can use the space bar to scroll through the remaining words.

Ask the Thesaurus for other suggestions. If you press Alt-T while you're in the Thesaurus screen, you'll be asked for a new word. Try typing in one of the suggested words on the screen. It may lead you to another word that will be just what you're looking for. An alternative is to type in another word of your own that you think will more closely approximate the meaning you're looking for. As soon as you press F10 again, the Thesaurus will examine your new word and come up with another list of possible synonyms. In this manner, you can work your way through dozens of possible word choices until you eventually find the one you're looking for.

If the Thesaurus can't help you with your word, don't give up. Think of a possible synonym and write it in your text; then call up the Thesaurus to check it. You may find that your second choice produces results.

Chapter 7

Merging Files

MultiMate Advantage II offers one of the most powerful file-merge programs of any word processor available today. You can create multiple letters and documents that are extremely useful for mailings, list generation, and other business applications.

File Merge can also be used to read external files and then merge information from those files into a document you're currently working on. With file merging, you can tap into the real power of *MultiMate Advantage II*.

There are essentially two types of merges: One occurs at printout, the other occurs onscreen while you're editing a document. We'll consider each separately.

Merging Onscreen

MultiMate Advantage II calls merging onscreen *external copying*. It merges information from an external document into the document you're currently working on.

For example, if you're writing a letter to someone and can't recall the person's address, using the file-merging feature, you can open up last month's letter document, isolate the name and address, and have that data merged into your current letter.

To merge onscreen:

- Open a current document.
- Place your cursor where you want to merge information from an external document.
- Press Shift-F8. A Merge Document selection screen appears.

```
DOCUMENT: c7                        ‖PAGE:    1‖LINE:   41‖COL:   16‖       EXTERNAL COPY
|1..........................................«
                         MERGING FILES - CHAPTER 7«
«
«
«
«
«
«
«
«
«
|1........................................................«
      MultiMate Advantage II offers one of the most powerful file
merge programs of any wordprocessor available today.  With it «
you can create multiple letters and documents that are
extremely useful in mailings, list generation and other
business uses. You can also use it to read external files and
merge information from those files into the document you are
currentlyworking on. With file merging, you can tap into the
real power of MultiMate Advantage II.«
«
              Drive:C                    Document:
              Path: \MM\
Press F10 when finished, ESC to cancel, F6 for Directory, F7 for TOC       Alt
```

Figure 7-1. Merge Document Screen

- Now enter the name and full path of the external document you want merged.
- If you can't remember the name of the document, but you can remember the directory:

    Enter the correct directory.

    Press F6. *MultiMate Advantage II* will display all the files available from that directory. (To copy from a table of contents, use F7.)

    Enter the name of the file to be merged.

- Press F10. The external document will appear onscreen and the words START COPY WHERE? will appear at the top right of your screen.
- You must now highlight the portion of the document you want merged.

    To highlight text:

    Use arrow keys to go to the beginning of the portion you want merged, and then mark it.

    Press F10. COPY WHAT? now appears at the top right of your screen.

    Move the cursor to the end of the block you want merged.

    Press F10. The block is now marked.

- When the appropriate block has been highlighted, press F10.

The block you highlighted will be copied into your current document file at the spot where you originally left your cursor.

To cancel the merge:
• Press Esc.

If you change your mind, you can cancel at any time *before* the final merge is executed. Once the file block has been merged, however, you can no longer cancel it, but you *can* erase all or a portion of the block that was merged in the usual manner.

```
DOCUMENT: c7                      ‖PAGE:   1‖LINE:  32‖COL:    1‖        INSERT
    MultiMate Advantage II offers one of the most powerful file
merge programs of any wordprocessor available today.  With it
you can create multiple letters and documents that are
extremely useful in mailings, list generation and other
business uses.«
«
    In this chapter, we'll consider several different editing
techniques that are both useful and sophisticated. While the
title of this chapter is ``Advanced Editing,'' there is nothing
esoteric or even complex about these techniques. Even the
complete beginner can pick them up after a few instructions.
What's advanced about these techniques is the way they function
within the word processor. In this chapter, we'll cover
columns, macros, footnotes, and formats.  «
«
«
«
    You can also use it to read external files and merge
information from those files into the document you are
currently working on.  «
«
    With file merging, you can tap into the real power of
MultiMate Advantage II.    There are essentially two types of
                                                             Alt
```

Figure 7-2. Example of a Block of Text Merged into a Current File

Merging at Printout

The second kind of merging available with *MultiMate Advantage II* does not occur onscreen, but happens at printout. It's most commonly used with a mailing list.

You create a master letter and a mailing list and have *MultiMate Advantage II* insert names, addresses, and other information into the letter from the mailing list. *MultiMate Advantage II* creates as many merged copies as you want, each with a different name and address.

Print merging is more complex than onscreen merging. It involves learning how to tell *MultiMate Advantage II* which information is to be merged in the master document (called a *merge file*) from the list (called a *list file,* or *merge data file*).

You can merge data from a wide variety of list files. These can be files you create or obtain externally that are in a variety of formats such as ASCII, dBASE, and others. The simplest merge is accomplished using a list you create.

Creating the Master Document

The Merge Document contains two elements: constants and variables. *Constants* are the portions of the letter you don't want to change; *variables* (or *merge items*) are those portions you do want to change. For example, in the following line, "NAME" is a variable and everything else is a constant.

We were so pleased that NAME could join us for the party.

In a merged document, a person's name from an external list is entered where the variable "NAME" appears onscreen, so that upon printout, the line may read something like this:

We were so pleased that Joan could join us for the party.

In each succeeding copy, a new name is substituted for the variable. Thus *MultiMate Advantage II* can quickly generate a large number of "personalized" documents.

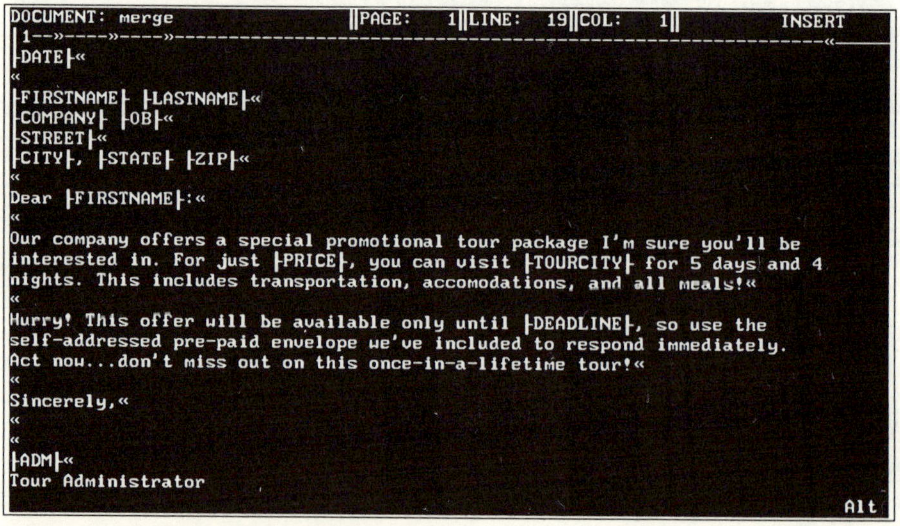

Figure 7-3. Typical Merge Document

```
DOCUMENT: list1                    ‖PAGE:    1‖LINE:    1‖COL:    8‖        INSERT
 1------------------------------------------------------------------------«-
┤FIRSTNAME├«
Alfred├«
«
┤LASTNAME├«
Robinson├«
«
┤STREET├«
329 Maple View Drive├«
«
┤CITY├«
Dearborn├«
«
┤STATE├«
CALIFORNIA├«
«
┤ZIP├«
96137├«
«
┤PRICE├«
$499├«
«
┤TOURCITY├«
                                                                            Alt
```

Figure 7-4. Typical List Document

```
Alfred Robinson
329 Maple View Drive
Dearborn, CA 96137

Dear Alfred:

Our company offers a special promotional tour package I'm sure you'll be
interested in. For just $499, you can visit London, England for 5 days and
4 nights. This includes transportation, accomodations, and all meals!

Hurry! This offer will be available only until September 30, so use the
self-addressed pre-paid envelope we've included to respond immediately.
Act now...don't miss out on this once-in-a-lifetime tour!

Sincerely,


Pete Hanson
Tour Administrator
```

Figure 7-5. The Resulting Printout

Creating a Merge Document

Variables in a *MultiMate Advantage II* Merge Document are indicated by ⊦. A variable (or *merge item*) can have any name up to 12 characters, in either upper- or lowercase.

To insert a variable:
- Press Alt-M when you reach a point in your text where you want to insert a variable. The merge code (⊦) will appear.
- Type in any descriptive name up to 12 characters long. For example (uppercase letters are used here to distinguish the variable for you):
⊦FIRSTNAME⊦

You can have as many variables as you want, and they can be placed anywhere in text. Also, *MultiMate Advantage II* automatically handles spacing, so the variable name doesn't have to be the same length as the list name.

> **TIP:** The same variable must be spelled exactly the same, including case, throughout your text. If there's any difference at all in spelling, *MultiMate Advantage II* will read it as a different variable.

Creating a List File

Merging requires two files. Once you have your document file, you must also have a list file from which *MultiMate Advantage II* can merge data.

To create a list file:
- Open a file in the normal way, giving it a name you'll later recognize as your list file—for example, "LISTONE." Since this will be the list file, don't type in any text.
- For each item in the list, you'll type in a variable, first, to identify the item. Type variables exactly as they appear in your document file. For example, for the first item, the variable might be ⊦COMPANY⊦. Don't forget to include the variable symbol (⊦) at the beginning and end of the name.
- Once you've typed the variable name, type out the list item

name. For example, the company name might be *Miller and Miller*. Enter this *directly below the variable* as follows:

    ⊦COMPANY⊦
    Miller and Miller⊦

Note that while the variable name must have the variable symbol both before and after it, the list name has the symbol only after it.

> **TIP:** You don't have to put the variables in the list file in the same order as they appear in the document. You can put them in any order.

Records

It's a good idea to think of the list document as containing individual *page records*. In other words, each page of the list document should be for a separate account. On the first page you might list the variables for one person; on the second page relist them for another person, and so forth.

MultiMate Advantage II will treat the first page as a separate record and use all the entries to replace the variables in the Merge Document. Then, when it prints the document a second time, it will take the variables from the second page, and so forth. If you mix variables for two documents on the same page, it may confuse *MultiMate Advantage II*.

Blank Spaces on a Merge Document

If there's an extra merge item on the list document that doesn't occur on the Merge Document, *MultiMate Advantage II* will ignore it. However, if there's a merge entry on the Merge Document and no corresponding merge item on the list document, you'll end up with an empty space.

For example, you may have the merge entry ⊦COMPANY⊦ on the Merge Document, but no company name for some of your addressees. For those people, there will be a blank space on the line where the company name should appear:

Jim Peters
2880 Ridgeway
San Francisco, CA.

To prevent blank lines:

• Place the code OB (Omit Blank) on any line in the Merge Document that a questionable merge entry is placed. For example, if you think some of the page records won't have company names, enter the merge entry in this fashion:
⊦COMPANY⊦ ⊦OB⊦

You only need to enter one such command per line for it to affect the entire line. If there's no company name, when *MultiMate Advantage II* sees the OB command, it will omit the line entirely without leaving a blank space.

Preview a Merge Document

Once you've completed both the Merge Document and the Merge File, your task is essentially complete. Since there's always the chance an error may have been introduced, preview the document without actually printing it.

To use the Preview function:

• Exit the document and call up *MultiMate Advantage II*'s Merge Print function (5) from the main menu.
• Enter the names of the merge and file documents.
• When you're asked how many pages to print, select the number for as many pages as you wish to preview.
• When the print modification screen comes up, be sure to select *Console* as the print option, which *will send the print material to the screen instead of the printer.*
• Press F10.

MultiMate Advantage II will now print to screen and you'll be able to see your document exactly the way the printout will look—and, if necessary, you can go back and correct any errors.

Entering Merge Items Yourself

Sometimes, instead of having a list to enter into a document, you want to enter the various merge items yourself on the keyboard.

For example, if you have three letters to write and you don't want to take the time to create a list file for just three letters, you can enter the information in the document file yourself.

To manually enter merge information:

• Create the document file in the normal fashion, including merge entry information. Do not create a list file.

- Print the document file using the merge facility (5 on the main menu).
- *MultiMate Advantage II* will pause each time it comes to a merge entry, and will ask you to supply the appropriate name.
- Type in the data.

Merge Printing

To merge print:

- Choose 5 from the main menu instead of using the normal print command.
- You'll be asked to enter two file names:
  Enter the Merge Document.
  Enter the Merge Data File (list file).
- Give the full path and directory.
- Select *Page Range* when asked for the *range of records* (how many record-pages to print).
- Press F10.
- The Document Print Options screen will appear. Complete the screen in the usual manner, being sure to return the print options from Console to Printer.
- Press F10. *MultiMate Advantage II* will now print merge the Merge Document File with the Merge Data File.

Merging Data Instead of Records

In addition to OB (Omit Blank), there are a number of other commands you can insert into a Merge Document to create special effects. Thus far we have described using the merge facility to merge an unlimited number of page records with a document.

For example: You have a list of 100 names and company descriptions, each on a separate List Document page. You also have a single Merge Document. You want to merge the 100 names with the single Merge Document 100 times so you'll end up with 100 personalized letters.

On the other hand, you may want to merge the other way around—where you have a single document that has 100 names on it. *MultiMate Advantage II* allows you to search and extract from each Merge Page/Record whatever information you want and then put that information into a single document.

To merge data into a single document:

- Create a Merge Document File in the usual way.
- Type in all *constant* material.
- Add the following commands where you want *MultiMate Advantage II* to begin searching the page/records in a list document:

  ├REPEAT:?┤

  You must replace the question mark, which represents *the number of records from which you want information to be extracted,* with a two-digit number.

  ├NEXT┤

  This tells *MultiMate Advantage II* to go to the next page as soon as it finishes searching the current record/page.

  ├NAME┤

  Insert the variable or variables you wish *MultiMate Advantage II* to extract. For example, you might list:

  ├FIRSTNAME┤ ├LASTNAME┤
  ├COMPANYNAME┤
  ├PHONE┤

  This listing is handled in the same manner as creating a regular Merge Document.

  ├END REPEAT┤

  This final command tells *MultiMate Advantage II* you've finished entering fields.

- Now print the file in the usual manner, giving the names of both the merge and list files.

MultiMate Advantage II will produce one document on which all first names, last names, company names, and phone numbers, will appear in as many page/records as you specified.

> **TIP:** Be sure *MultiMate Advantage II* is in Insert mode to ensure that it won't overprint material that has already been typed in.

Repeated Printing of a Field from a Single Record

The following steps are used when you want information from only one page record repeated several times, instead of information extracted from several different page/records.

To repeat printing of a field from a single record:

- Follow the steps for merging data into a single document.
- Type in ⊦REPEAT:?⊦. The question mark represents *the number of times you want the fields to repeat on the same Merge Document.*
- Omit the ⊦NEXT⊦ command.
- Proceed as above for the remainder of the document.

At print-merge time, *MultiMate Advantage II* will repeat the field of the first page record as many times as you indicated. If you selected more than one page at the Print Merge menu, it will print out the fields as many times as selected for each page.

Programming Merge File

Thus far we have dealt with basic commands, although it's possible to program Merge to accomplish a wide variety of tasks. To do this, you'll need to know a number of new specialized terms:

Define	Tells *MultiMate Advantage II* that what follows is a special block of information to be used to define the list merge file.
File Type	You must tell *MultiMate Advantage II* the type of file that will be affected by the block commands. There are four file types available:

MULTIMATE	The file type we've used so far.
dBASE	An imported .dbf dBASE file.
Random	For a Random ASCII file.
Sequential	For a Sequential ASCII file.

End Define	This says the special block has ended; it completes the defined block's parameters.
Printif	Tells *MultiMate Advantage II* to print certain fields only if specific parameters are matched. For example, a typical Printif statement might be, PRINTIF NAME EQ(UALS) SMITH. Only those people with the last name of Smith will be printed out.
EQ	Equal to.
GE	Greater than or equal to.
GT	Greater than.
LE	Less than or equal to.
LT	Less than.
NE	Not equal to.

These commands allow *MultiMate Advantage II* to search each record and determine what's to be printed and what's to be eliminated. For that reason, the defined block containing these specialized commands must be at the very beginning of the Document Merge file.

Here are two examples of the use of these commands:

```
|DEFINE|  Line 1
FILE TYPE MULTIMATE <  Line 2
PRINTIF NAME EQ "SMITH" <  Line 3
PRINTIF CITY LE "NEW YORK" <  Line 4
|END DEFINE|  Line 5
```

This block tells *MultiMate Advantage II* to print all records containing the name *Smith* that also contain the city *New York* or any city whose name follows New York alphabetically.

```
|DEFINE|  Line 1
FILE TYPE MULTIMATE <  Line 2
PRINTIF NAME GT "SMITH" LT THAN "JONES" CITY NE
"NEW YORK"
|END DEFINE|  Line 4
```

This block tells *MultiMate Advantage II* to print all records preceding *Jones* and following *Smith* alphabetically, in all cities except New York.

Note: Be sure you put the record reference in quotation marks or MultiMate Advantage II *won't be able to tell it apart from the commands.*

Importing Merge Lists from Other Programs

You can import lists directly from any *dBase* program, and you can import any list from another program that has first been converted to ASCII code (either random or sequential).

Importing from *dBase* Files

To import from a *dBase* file:

• Create a defined block at the beginning of the Merge Document File. It should look like the following:

```
├DEFINE┤ Line 1
FILE TYPE DBASE Line 2
├END DEFINE┤ Line 3
```

• You may now import directly from a *dBase* file.

> **TIP:** Printif statements probably won't work here. Also, beware of underlined words—they mean something different to *MultiMate Advantage II* than they did to *dBase*. It's best to avoid underlining in the dBASE list file. If you do use underline, enclose the word in merge symbols.

Importing ASCII Files

ASCII is the standard code used by all computers. There are two types of ASCII files: *sequential* and *random*.

In the sequential file, *delimiters* are used to identify fields; typically, these are quotation marks. A field in a sequential file might look like this:

"Henry Smith Corporation",

In a random file, no such delimiters are used. A field in a random file might look like this:

Henry Smith Corporation,

You must specify whether the file is sequential or random so *MultiMate Advantage II* can tell where the fields are located. If you're using a sequential file, you simply indicate the various fields you're going to use:

```
├DEFINE┤ LINE 1
FILE TYPE SEQUENTIAL LINE 2
FIELD NAME FIRST LINE 3
FIELD NAME SECOND LINE 4
FIELD NAME THIRD LINE 5
├END DEFINE┤ LINE 6
```

> **TIP:** *MultiMate Advantage II* always assumes the *delimiter* is a quotation mark (''), the *field separator* is the comma (,), and the *record separator* is the Return.
>
> If the merge file uses symbols other than these, you must tell *MultiMate Advantage II* in the defined block. For example,
>
> **FIELD DELIMITER %**
>
> tells *MultiMate Advantage II* that the delimiter is the percent symbol.

If you're using a random file, you must tell *MultiMate Advantage II* the maximum length of each field so it won't inadvertently blend information from several fields. A random file would look essentially the same as a sequential, except the size of the field would be given. For example,

```
|DEFINE| LINE1 FILE TYPE RANDOM LINE 2
FIELD NAME FIRST SIZE 15 LINE 3
FIELD NAME SECOND SIZE 10 LINE 4
|DEFINE END| LINE 5
```

This tells *MultiMate Advantage II* that the first field is 15 characters long and the second field is 10 characters long.

> **TIP:** If a field contains spaces, enclose the field in the merge symbols,
>
> |FIRST NAME|
>
> or it will confuse *MultiMate Advantage II*.

Chapter 8
Printing Techniques

The purpose of using a word processor, ultimately, is to get a printout. In this chapter, we'll look at various techniques for making the printout look like the screen. Even more important, we'll consider methods of modifying the document so its printout will appear exactly as you want it.

Printer Considerations

Today there are essentially three types of printers available: impact (letter quality), dot-matrix, and laser. Each has different print capabilities.

Impact. An impact uses a daisy wheel or similar device to create characters on paper. Similar to a typewriter, the letter is impacted onto a ribbon that strikes the paper. In terms of attributes, you're limited to the characters that exist on your wheel. To get a different typeface, for example, you must stop the printer and switch wheels.

MultiMate Advantage II, however, can create certain simple features, such as boldface or underlining, by striking characters twice or by going back and underlining a character.

Dot-Matrix. These printers create the characters from computer memory, using a matrix of anywhere from 9 to 24 character pins. Dot-matrix printers are limited to the typefaces and their enhancements contained within the printer's memory. *MultiMate Advantage II* can access the various dot-matrix print enhancements and normally create a wide variety of print attributes, including boldface, underline, enlarge, condense, and superscript/subscript.

Laser Printers. These printers are similar to copy machines, but they're much more sophisticated. In addition to its printing facility, a laser printer also contains a computer in which various complete typefaces or *fonts* are stored (or loaded). The fonts contain all the characters and numerals for a variety of typefaces. The big difference—in terms of controlling the printer—between dot-matrix and laser printers is that while dot-matrix printers can be directed to modify a particular typeface to create a print attribute, a laser printer must contain that attribute within the font.

For example, to get italics using a dot-matrix printer, *MultiMate Advantage II* sends the printer the code for italics and then continues to send the commands for normal characters. To print the word *attribute* in italics, the command to turn on the italics function is sent and the characters are sent, and then the command to turn off the italics function is sent. The printer receives these commands; when called upon to turn on italics, it slants its normal typeface, thus giving it an italic appearance.

On the other hand, when the command for italics is received by a laser printer, it switches from a roman (nonitalic font) to a separate font in which all characters are italic. If the printer doesn't have an italic font, it can't switch.

The same is true for boldface and the other print attributes. Bold is achieved in one of three ways on a dot-matrix printer: by repeatedly striking the character over, by moving the print head slightly up or down and restriking, or by moving the print head slightly left or right and restriking. Bold is achieved on a laser printer by switching to a bold font (if available). The print attributes you ultimately get are determined by your printer—and by installing the correct printer driver from *MultiMate Advantage II*.

Printer Drivers (Communicating with the Printer)

MultiMate Advantage II offers drivers for the most popular printers on the market. When you install the program (see the Appendix), you'll select a driver for your printer. Drivers are called *Printer Action Tables (PATs),* and are set up to tell *MultiMate Advantage II* which commands to send to your printer to activate its various functions. In terms of laser printers, PATs also contain character width tables and other information.

In addition to PATs, *MultiMate Advantage II* includes a variety of *Sheet Feeder Action Tables (SATs),* which allow the use of certain sheet feeders with your printer, where applicable. In order to get your printer to operate, you must install the correct PAT (and SAT, if needed). Once installed, the PAT will be available to *MultiMate Advantage II*; when you print, it will translate onscreen commands to the correct printer codes and make your hardcopy just the way you want it.

Print Attributes

Many people think *print attributes* (such as boldface and underline) that appear onscreen are simply transferred directly from the screen to the printer. Technically speaking, that's not the case. To get print attributes, special codes must be sent from your computer to your printer. More important, not all printers are capable of printing out all print attributes you see onscreen. In fact, some of the more primitive printers can print very few attributes, so there are really two parts to the problem of getting what you want from your printer: communicating the correct code from your computer (and from *MultiMate Advantage II*) and obtaining a printer that can deliver the kind of printout you want.

Let's now take a look at the specific attributes you can insert into your text.

Boldface

Dot-matrix printers strike twice for boldface; laser printers switch to a bold font.

To activate boldface:

- Press Alt-Z to turn on boldface.
- Type in the text you want to appear in boldface.
- Press Alt-Z again to turn off boldface.

A textured rectangle will appear onscreen indicating where bold has been turned on. A similar rectangle will appear, indicating where bold was turned off. Everything between the two rectangles will be in boldface.

Note: You can enter boldfacing either before or after typing.

It's important to understand that text onscreen will not become bolder; rather, the boldfacing will take place on the printout. If you wish to remove boldfacing, simply delete the symbol. Remember to delete turn-on *and* turn-off boldfacing symbols. If you delete only one symbol, the remaining one will turn on the boldface, producing an undesirable printout.

Letter-Quality (Enhanced)

If you have a dot-matrix printer, you can switch to letter-quality print with this command. If your dot-matrix printer doesn't have a letter-quality function, *MultiMate Advantage II* will double-strike the print, creating an effect almost identical to bold.

To activate letter-quality:

• Press Alt-N to turn on letter-quality.
• Type in the text you want to print as letter-quality.
• Press Alt-N again to turn it off.

The symbol ∩ will appear onscreen when the command is used to turn the letter-quality function on and off. Everything between the symbols will be in letter-quality, although the screen display characters do not change their appearance. You can turn on letter-quality either while typing or by adding the symbol afterward.

To return to draft quality:

• Press Alt-D. This turns on draft and removes letter quality.

Shadow Printing

MultiMate Advantage II offers a type of gray printing called *shadow* that's useful with large letters. Dot-matrix printers actually screen the print so it has a "toned" effect.

To activate shadow:

• Press Alt-X to turn shadow on.
• Use Alt-X a second time to turn it off.

A double–vertical-line symbol will be entered into the text. All text between the double–vertical-line symbols will be in shadow. You may enter text before or after you've created the shadow symbols. To remove shadow printing, delete the symbols. (Remember to delete *both* symbols.)

Underlining

MultiMate Advantage II handles underlining as a graphic element rather than as a print attribute; however, because underlining is commonly considered an attribute, we'll discuss it in this section.

To underline existing text:

• Press Shift-− (minus sign). Use the character keys, not the numeric keypad.

On a monochrome monitor, underlining should appear onscreen. On a color monitor, a different color should appear, depending on how you set up the monitor during installation.

To type everything in underline mode:

• Press Alt-+ (plus sign). Use the character keys, not the numeric keypad. Now, whatever you type will automatically be underlined.
• Repeat the procedure to turn off underlining.

To delete underlining from an individual character:

• Place the cursor on the character.
• Press Shift-− (minus sign).

To underline only characters and not numbers:

• Press Alt-− (minus sign). Use the character keys, not the numeric keypad.

To double underline:

• Press Ctrl-− (minus sign). Use the character keys, not the numeric keypad.

To turn off double underline:

• Repeat the procedure for double underlining. A vertical arrow will appear.
• Delete the vertical arrow to remove the double underline. Remember to remove both the turn-on and turn-off arrows.

Superscript/Subscript

To turn on or off superscript:

• Press Alt-Q.

To turn on or off subscript.

• Press Alt-W.

Pitch

In addition to the normal attributes already covered, *MultiMate Advantage II* provides the opportunity to set the print *pitch*. The command is handled in the same manner as a normal print attribute.

To change the print pitch:

- Press Alt-C. A letter *P* appears with an arrow next to it.
- Now type in the print pitch you wish to use.

Note: MultiMate Advantage II will attempt to accommodate your choice of pitch; however, it's ultimately up to your printer's capabilities. If your printer cannot print the pitch you've selected, MultiMate Advantage II will attempt to print the nearest possible pitch.

MultiMate Advantage II uses a special print pitch code command for setting pitch. The code should be entered directly after the print pitch symbol.

Table 8-1. Print Pitch Codes

	Characters Per Inch	Code
Smaller	17.6	9
	16.5	8
	15	7
	13.2	6
	12	5
	10	4
	8.5	3
	6	2
Bigger	5	1

Font Selection

Font selection is primarily used for laser printers. Instead of using the various print attribute commands discussed so far, if you have a laser printer, chances are you'll work almost exclusively with print *fonts*.

To use the following command, you must have a PAT that offers various print fonts installed.

To access print fonts:

- Press Alt-C.

This is the same command used for accessing print pitches, so the same *P* with the arrow will appear onscreen. Now, however, instead of using the number code to indicate pitch, use a letter code to indicate the font you want.

To see which fonts are available from your PAT:

• Press Alt-C and a question mark (?).

A list of all the print fonts available will appear onscreen. If you have no other fonts available for your printer other than your current one, the message NO FONTS AVAILABLE FOR THE SPECIFIED PAT will appear.

TIP: It may be possible to use a different PAT for your printer — one with a greater font selection. Try selecting PATs for similar printers, and then run a trial printout to see what works best.

Note: It's possible to change the Printer Action Table to accommodate your printer's specific needs. This will be discussed at the end of the chapter.

To return to the original font:

• Unlike other print attributes, you cannot repeat the original procedure to return to the original font; instead, you must change fonts. If you were using the *A* font and then changed to the *F* font, use must change back to the *A* font.

TIP: You may have a laser printer that accommodates many different fonts. A PAT, however, can handle only 26; therefore, you may want to create several different PATs for your printer.

Custom User Codes

MultiMate Advantage II also allows you to send your own printer codes. This is particularly helpful with dot-matrix printers when you want to send a code telling the printer to switch to a particular function that wasn't included in the PAT.

It's important to understand that using custom codes is one of the more sophisticated functions of *MultiMate Advantage II* and requires at least a basic understanding of ASCII code procedures.

To send ASCII code directly to the printer:

• Press Alt-A. An ASCII symbol will appear.
• Type in the code you want, using *decimal* equivalents.

This procedure can be used to have your printer type in symbols not found within *MultiMate Advantage II*'s normal keyboards. It can also be used to turn on or off various printer functions. If you want to use custom codes to control printer functions, examine the documentation that came with your printer to decide which ASCII codes you want to use.

Printer documentation normally gives the codes in *hexadecimal* and *decimal* equivalents. Use the decimal equivalents. Printer function codes (such as a carriage return) are usually in the first 33 numbers of ASCII (or a combination of one of the first 33 plus another number). If you want to use other symbols, use a chart of ASCII symbol equivalents.

```
DOCUMENT: c8                    ||PAGE:   17||LINE:   32||COL:   38||        HOTPRINTING
symbols, then use a chart of ASCII symbol equivalents.«
«
    INSERT CHART OF ASCII SYMBOL EQUIVALENTS«
«
«
«
«
«
TO PRINT«
«
    Printing out  is a relatively simple procedure with«
«
MultiMate Advantage II.  There is a "hot print" which takes«
«
«
GETTING THE MOST OUT OF MULTIMATE ADVANTAGE II - PAGE 14«
«
«
«
«
«
«
«
                                                              Ctrl
```

Figure 8-1. Hot Print Screen

Printing

Printing out a document is a fairly simple procedure with *MultiMate Advantage II*. *Hot Print* takes advantage of the DOS screen dump command to print any screen page; *Normal* print allows you to set the print parameters.

To engage Hot Print:

(Be sure you have the correct text onscreen.)

• Press Ctrl–Print Screen. The current page will be printed.

   Note: Using Hot Print, you cannot stop the printer action from the program until the entire page has been printed. If you must stop the printer, turn it off.

To engage Normal Print:

(Printing is accessed from the main menu. You must exit a document before you can print it.)

• Select number 3 from the main menu in order to print. The program will ask what document you want to print.
• Type in the document name, giving full drive and path information. (You can print a table of contents as well as a document.)

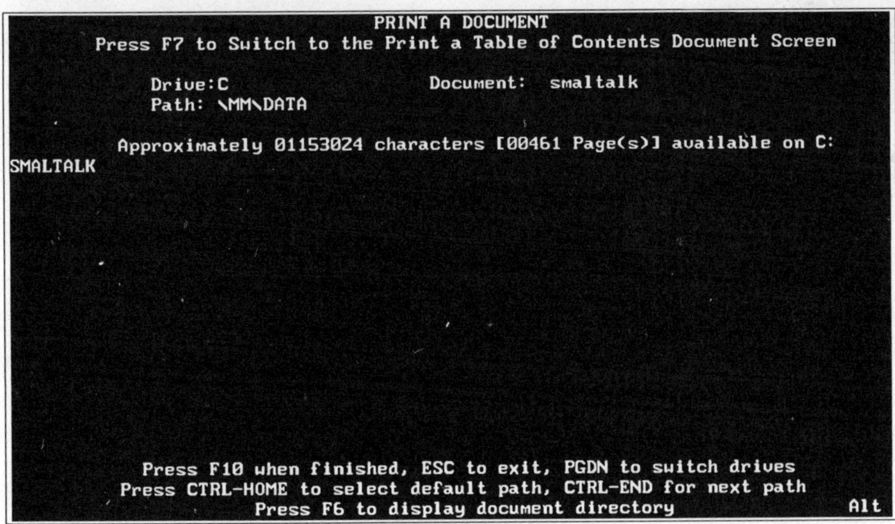

Figure 8-2. Print A Document Menu

The Document Print Options screen will appear. This is a full-powered screen with dozens of options. If this is the first time you're printing, don't let the screen confuse you. In most cases, you can simply press F10 to select the defaults and bypass the screen. In other cases, you'll want to change one or more of the defaults to correspond with the type of printout you desire. Use the arrow keys to move through the screen.

```
Document:  SMTKL3          DOCUMENT PRINT OPTIONS

Start Print At Page Number        001  Left Margin                         000
Stop Print After Page Number      001  Top Margin                          000
Enhanced [N] / Draft [Y]            N  Double Space The Document [N or Y]     N
Number Of Original Copies         001  Default Pitch [4 = 10 CPI]             4

Printer Action Table (PAT)    TTYCRLF  Sheet Feeder Action Table(SAT)
Use:(P)arallel/(S)erial/(F)ile/(L)ist  Sheet Feeder Bin Numbers [0 - 3]
    (A)uxiliary/(C)onsole           P     First Page 0  Middle 0  Last Page 0
Device Number                     001  Char. Width/Translate (CWT)
Pause Between Pages [N or Y]         N  Background / Foreground [B or F]       B

Print Comments [N or Y]             N  Justification [N or Y or (M)icro]     N
Print Doc. Summary Screen [N or Y]  N  Proportional Spacing [N or Y]         N
Print This Screen [N or Y]           N  Lines Per Inch [6 or 8]               6
Header / Footer First Page Number 001  Paper Length (lines per page)       066
Starting Footnote Number[1 - 749] 001  Default Font                          A
                                       Remove Queue Entry When Done [Y or N] Y

Current Time Is     16:25:08           Delay Print Until Time Is    16:25:08
Current Date Is     06/30/1988         Delay Print Until Date Is    06/30/1988

              Press F10 when finished, ESC to exit
              Press F1 for PATs, F2 for SATs, F3 for CWTs              Alt
```

Figure 8-3. Document Print Options Screen

Start/Stop Prints

To start printing at any time while in the Document Print Options screen:

• Press F10. This immediately engages the printer driver which sends the file to the printer.

To stop printing:

• Press the Ctrl and Break (Pause) keys simultaneously. (The Break key is usually on or near the numeric keypad.)

This calls up the Printer Queue Control menu. (See Figure 8-6.) The document you're printing will stop. Selection number 5 on this menu will restart the print. Any other selection will abort the print, but won't cancel the printing of other files you've already queued up.

You can only pause and then continue printing by using the printer's own controls.

To pause printing:

• Press the Online button found on most printers. This will take the printer offline, causing it to pause.

An error message, PRINTER NEEDS ATTENTION, will eventually appear onscreen, which tells you that *MultiMate Advantage II* has disengaged from sending the printer information.

• Press Esc.

You may now use *MultiMate Advantage II* to edit another document or perform any other function that doesn't involve printing the document.

To resume printing:

• Return the printer to online status.

TIP: Many printers contain *buffers,* which store a page or more of memory. This allows the computer to quickly feed information to the printer and allows the printer to absorb information at its own rate. When you cancel printing (Ctrl-Break), the computer will immediately stop sending information to the printer. If the printer already has a full buffer, however, it may continue to print a page or more before stopping. The same thing may happen if you pause and then decide to cancel.

To avoid this problem when you want to immediately halt printing, turn your printer off and use the keyboard controls.

To pause printing from inside a document:

• Press Alt-P. A small "house" symbol (⌂) will appear onscreen to show where you've paused.

You may add as many of these as you wish throughout the

text. When the printer encounters one of the symbols, it will receive the signal to pause.

To resume printing:

• Press Esc. The printer will begin where it left off.

Number of Pages

Indicate the starting page number and the ending page number. You're limited to 254 pages of printing per document. If you have more than that, divide your document into two files and print each separately. If you wish to print only the first page, enter 001 for both first and last page. You may begin printing on any page of the document you like.

Note: Page numbers correspond to the onscreen pages. Be sure you repaginate your document before printing out.

Enhanced/Draft

This control asks whether you want the document printed in letter quality or draft quality. Its operation depends on the printer you have. In many cases, letter quality will turn out to be nothing more than boldface. A little experimenting will quickly tell you which is true for your printer.

To engage letter or draft quality:

• The default is *N* for letter quality.
• Type *Y* for draft quality.

Number of Copies

The default is 1. You may enter the number of copies you wish to print, up to 254.

Printer Action Table (PAT)

You must enter the Printer Action Table you originally installed for your printer. If you enter the wrong PAT, you won't get a proper printout. F1 indicates the PATs that are available.

> **TIP:** You may be able to use more than one PAT for your printer. You'll have to experiment to find out. The Epson EPFXLINE.PAT, for example, which comes with *MultiMate Advantage II,* can be used instead of the standard EPSON.PAT file to get line drawing capabilities with Epson printers (except 24-pin models).

Left Margin

Print margins are set at the time of printing, not from within the document itself. Setting the left margin will also set the right margin.

To set the left margin:

- Determine the line length in inches. The default length is 7.5 inches. As an example, if you want to reset the line length to 6.5 inches and your page is a standard 8.5 inches wide, that leaves 2 inches for margins.

  To set a 1-inch print margin on each side of the page:

  Set the left margin at 1 inch. One inch plus the 6.5 inches of your text equals 7.5 inches. Subtract that from the page width of 8.5 inches and you get a 1-inch right margin (1 + 6.5 + 1 = 8.5). The margin is set in characters per inch, so in order to get a 1-inch margin, you must determine the pitch of the typeface and then enter the appropriate number of characters. For example, if you're using 12 pitch, there are 12 characters to an inch, so entering the number 012 will give you a 1-inch margin. Entering 006 will give you a half-inch margin.

Top Margin

Setting the top margin for the page will also set the bottom margin. The formula is

Top Margin + Lines of Type − Total Lines on Page = Bottom Margin

The top margin is set in lines: 003 equals three lines, 004 equals four lines, and so forth. To convert lines to inches, determine how many lines per inch you set up for your document. If you set three lines per inch (double spacing), three lines at the top will equal one inch.

Additional Print Options

So far, we've discussed the most commonly set parameters for printing. However, you may wish to reset the remaining parameters on the Document Print screen.

Use. This allows you to determine the method of transmission of your document to the printer.

Serial	Sends the data via your designated serial port.
Parallel	Sends the data via your designated parallel port.
List	Sends the data to a parallel listed port other than the designated parallel port. (You must select a different port using the operating system. See your DOS manual.)
Auxiliary	Sends the data to a serial port other than the designated serial port. (You must select a different serial port using the operating system. See your DOS manual.)
Console	Sends the printed document to the screen instead of to the printer. This will allow you to preview the entire document instead of a page, as with the normal preview function.
File	Creates an ASCII file. This is very important if you wish to convert *MultiMate Advantage II* documents to a standard format that can then be read by another word processor. When you use File, your document will be re-created with the same name but with a .PRN extension on the same disk as the original.

Device Number. Indicate your output port here. Using just one printer, the designation should be 001.

Pause Between Pages. If you want to insert a new piece of paper after each page, enter *Y(es)*.

Print Comments. These are comments to yourself or to other users of the file that normally wouldn't be printed. Comments are entered into text by placing them between exclamation marks:

!! (Enter)
COMMENTS
!! (Enter)

Entering *Y(es)* here will allow these comments to be printed; *N(o)* will leave them out.

Print Screens. You can choose to print the document summary and/or the print option screen.

Headers / Footers. This allows you to change the automatic numbering provided you have

- used a header or a footer
- placed a number in the header or footer
- used the Automatic Page Number system (#); when creating a header or footer, pressing Shift-3 will enter this symbol.

You can select the page number to replace the first pound (#) symbol by entering that number here.

Note: This will not work with the System Page Numbering Method 24.

Pitch. Set the pitch here. This is the pitch the printer will first use to begin the document. If you set different pitches inside the document, this will be changed as the printer comes to those commands. (See the section on pitch in this chapter.)

Sheet Feeder Action Table. Indicate the SAT, if any, you're using here. (See the section on SATs in this chapter.)

Character Width Translation Table. If you created a special CWT table, you can list it here. (See the section on character width translation in this chapter.)

Background / Foreground. This allows you to print and to continue working. Select *B(ackground)* for this option. To print only, select *F(oreground)*.

Justification. This is a complex setting and what you select will depend a great deal on your printer's capabilities.

To achieve a "ragged right" effect (similar to typewriter text):
  Select *N* for No Justification.

To achieve a justified, "flush right and flush left," margin:
  Select *Y* for Justification.

```
     This is an example of justified
type.  Note  that both margins are even.
All  the  characters end both flush left
and  flush right. Justified text  is
typically used  for publications. It is
rarely    used    for    correspondence.

     This is an example of a ragged
right, flush left margin. The
characters on the left are flush while
those on the right have a sawtooth
edge. This is the type of text
typically used for correspondence.
```

Figure 8-4. Examples of Ragged Right and Justified Text

The problem with simple justified text is that to create a flush margin on both left and right sides, *MultiMate Advantage II* must add spaces between words, resulting in an awkward appearance.

To make text look more polished, it's possible to add spaces between the letters within words as well as between the words themselves. This is called *microjustification* and it may or may not be available with your printer.

To activate microjustification:
• Type *M*.

If your printer doesn't handle microjustification, it will present you with standard justification.

Proportional Spacing. As a further step toward truly professional appearing type, the printer can assign different widths for different characters.

For those unfamiliar with the need for proportional spacing, consider the letters *M* and *I*. Normally the letter *M* takes up twice as much space as the letter *I*. However, in normal *monospacing,* such as found on most typewriters, each character is given the same amount of space, so words with thin letters look too widely spaced while words with fatter letters look too cramped. Proportional spacing allows only as much space as is needed for each letter within a word, and as a result, presents a highly polished manuscript appearance.

You can turn on proportional spacing by selecting *Y(es)*; however, if your printer doesn't support proportional spacing, you won't notice any difference in the printout. Only if your printer supports proportional spacing will you be able to detect the difference.

```
     This is an example of proportional
spacing. The letters are each given
only as much room as they need. An "I"
is given less room, for example, than
an "A."


             This  is  an  example  of
non-proportional  spacing.  The  letters
are  each given the same amount of room,
regardless  of their size. An "I" and an
"A"  are  given  exactly  the same room.
```

Figure 8-5. Example of Proportional and Nonproportional Spacing

Lines and Length. Set the lines per inch and the lines per page here; 66 is the normal number of lines for an 11-inch high page.

Font. (Used mostly by laser printers.) Set the font the document will begin with. You may change fonts within a document as described earlier.

Queuing. *MultiMate Advantage II* was originally designed to be a multiuser, multidocument program. It's designed to allow for the printing of a number of documents sequentially (for example, the chapters in a book) as well as to delay the printing until a time when the computer system is used less.

Documents are entered into the queue in the order in which they're sent to the printer. The queue lines up the documents and prints them one at a time. The default setting (Y) is to remove the document once it has been printed. This can be changed so the document will again queue up, although it will be placed in a holding status.

Time/Date Print Delay. The time displayed depends on the time you entered when you began the program (or the time that was entered automatically for you from DOS). If you skipped the time entry, the display will be empty.

You can set the time you want your document to be printed by indicating the hour, minute, and second. The date can be set in the same manner.

Changing the Defaults

It's possible to change the standard defaults that appear on the Document Print Options menu. If there are other defaults you would rather have, these can be inserted.

For example, if you would rather have the Document Print

Options screen, use Draft instead of Enhanced as the default; you can make that change from anywhere in the program *except while printing is on hold* or *while there's an error message onscreen.*

To change the default settings:

• Choose Additional Print Functions from the main menu.
• Type 2 (Edit Printer Defaults). This allows you to edit the Document Print Options screen. Go through the various categories and make the changes you want.

Note: The changes you make will be permanent until you replace them again.

```
                        EDIT PRINTER DEFAULTS

Start Print At Page Number          001   Left Margin                          000
Stop Print After Page Number        999   Top Margin                           000
Enhanced [N] / Draft [Y]              N   Double Space The Document [N or Y]     N
Number Of Original Copies           001   Default Pitch [4 = 10 CPI]             4

Printer Action Table (PAT)   TTYCRLF      Sheet Feeder Action Table(SAT)
Use:(P)arallel/(S)erial/(F)ile/(L)ist     Sheet Feeder Bin Numbers [0 - 3]
    (A)uxiliary/(C)onsole           P         First Page 0  Middle 0  Last Page 0
Device Number                       001   Char. Width/Translate (CWT)
Pause Between Pages [N or Y]          N   Background / Foreground [B or F]       B

Print Comments [N or Y]               N   Justification [N or Y or (M)icro]     N
Print Doc. Summary Screen [N or Y]    N   Proportional Spacing [N or Y]         N
Print This Screen [N or Y]            N   Lines Per Inch [6 or 8]               6
Header / Footer First Page Number 001     Paper Length (lines per page)       066
Starting Footnote Number[1 - 749] 001     Default Font                          A
                                          Remove Queue Entry When Done [Y or N] Y



                  Press F10 when finished, ESC to exit
                  Press F1 for PATs, F2 for SATs, F3 for CWTs              All
```

Figure 8-6. Edit Printer Defaults Screen

Controlling the Print Queue

You can send a large number of documents to the printer, one after the other, without waiting for them to be printed. They're held in place and lined up in the print queue.

MultiMate Advantage II allows easy access to the queue controls if you want to change the order in which the documents are printed, or if you want to put a document on hold or delete it entirely from the print queue.

To control the print queue:

- Choose Additional Print Functions from the main menu.
- Select 1 for Printer Queue Control.

```
                    PRINTER QUEUE CONTROL

          1) Remove a Document from the Queue
          2) Place a Document on Hold
          3) Release a Document from Hold
          4) Move a Document to the top of the Queue
          5) Restart the Document Currently Printing

   C4          C6          C7




          File Status:   Printing   Hold   Errors will Blink
                  (* indicates Table of Contents)
                Place the cursor next to the document name
     Press the numeric key (1 to 5) for the function to be performed
                        Press ESC to exit
```

Figure 8-7. Printer Queue Control Menu

The Printer Queue Control menu allows the following operations:

- Delete a document from the queue (it no longer will be printed).
- Hold a document so you can edit it before printing.
- Put a document that has been on hold back into the queue.
- Change the position of a document by indicating that it's the next to be printed.
- Abort the document currently being printed and restart it.

Below the menu, all the documents in the queue will be listed. Those on hold will be shown in reverse video while the document currently printed will be highlighted. Documents containing errors will blink.

Printing Errors

If you have a problem with the printer or other hardware, or if you incorrectly entered information in the Document Print Options screen, a document you sent to the printer may show up in the Queue but may be unprintable. Those documents that are unprintable because of errors will be listed below the Printer Queue Control menu and will blink.

Select 1 to remove the document. If the document remains in the queue despite repeated attempts to remove it, that document has jammed the queue software. To remove the document, you must remove the file in which it resides, which is called WPQUE.SYS. It must be removed from the DOS operating system after exiting *MultiMate Advantage II*.

Additional Print Considerations

In addition to the various print techniques discussed so far, there are additional considerations that tend to be more technical in nature. Some may require minimal programming skills.

Special Characters

In addition to the regular characters available from your keypad, there are additional characters you can send to your printer.

To send any ASCII character to the printer from the keypad:

• Press Alt-C and then the decimal equivalent.

Certain special characters can be sent to the printer from within a document using one of the five alternate keyboards provided with *MultiMate Advantage II* (Figure 8-8).

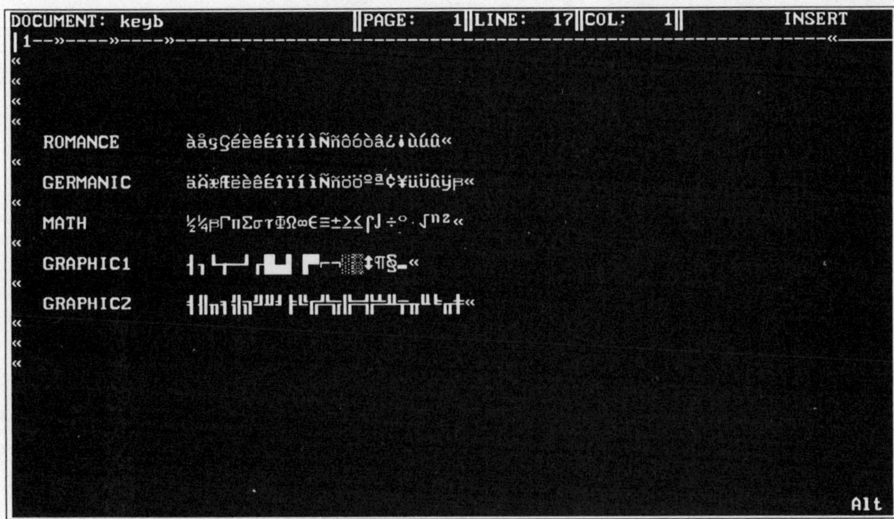

Figure 8-8. Alternate Keyboards with Keys

To access the alternate keyboards:

• Press Alt-K. The current selection will momentarily appear in the upper right-hand corner of the screen.

To change the selection:

• Repeat the process. You can quickly move through the entire menu.

Modifying the Printer Action Table

The PAT determines which codes will be sent to your printer. Generally speaking, codes above decimal 033 are screen characters; those below are functions (such as backspacing).

The PAT controls all of these, translating the codes from *MultiMate Advantage II* into the codes your printer understands. If the PAT doesn't operate all the functions of your printer, or if there's some rearrangement of codes you would like to make, you can modify the PAT.

To modify the PAT:

• From the Opening Menu, select the Utilities menu.
• Select Printer Tables Editor from the Utilities menu. From this menu you can edit the PAT, SAT, or CWT tables. The proce-

dure for each is essentially the same, so we'll concentrate on editing the PAT.

- Select the PAT menu for editing. You'll be asked to select the PAT you wish to edit (those available will be listed).
- Only PATs you've installed will be shown.

Note: If the PAT you wish to edit is not shown, you'll have to exit the table editing program and install the PAT you want.

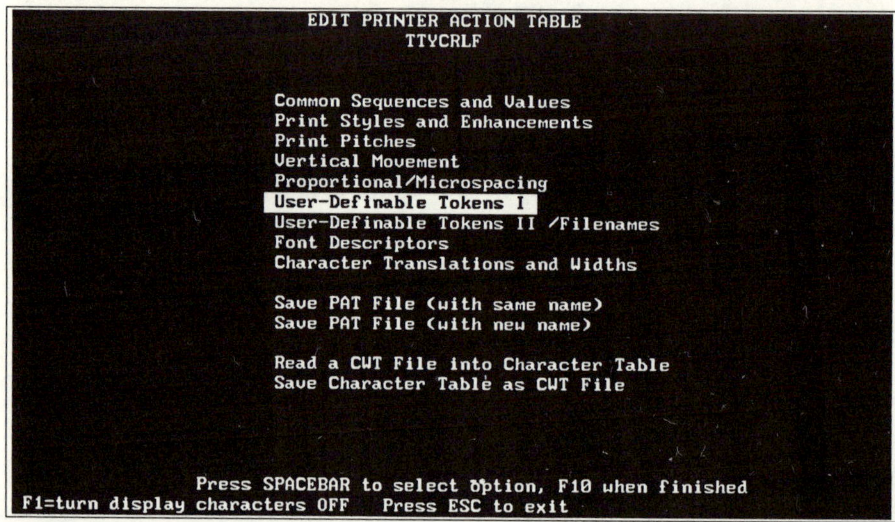

Figure 8-9. Edit Printer Action Table Screen

TIP: If you're an advanced user, you can create your own PAT from scratch.

To create your own PAT:

- Select the Create PAT table option from the PAT menu.

```
EDIT PRINTER ACTION TABLE            TTYCRLF        Character Translations/Widths
   F2 will change input mode to ASCII
   CHAR TRANSL WD    CHAR TRANSL WD    CHAR TRANSL WD    CHAR TRANSL WD
   00    000000  0   01 ☺ 000000  0    02 ☻ 000000  0   03 ♥ 000000  0
   04 ♦ 000000  0    05 ♣ 000000  0    06 ♠ 000000  0   07 · 000000  0
   08 ▫ 000000  0    09 ○ 000000  0    0A ◙ 000000  0   0B ♂ 000000  0
   0C ♀ 000000  0    0D ♪ 000000  0    0E ♫ 000000  0   0F ☼ 000000  0
   10 ► 000000  0    11 ◄ 000000  0    12 ↕ 000000  0   13 ‼ 000000  0
   14 ¶ 000000  0    15 § 000000  0    16 ▬ 000000  0   17 ↨ 000000  0
   18 ↑ 000000  0    19 ↓ 000000  0    1A → 000000  0   1B ← 000000  0
   1C └ 000000  0    1D ↔ 000000  0    1E ▲ 000000  0   1F ▼ 000000  0
   20   000000  0    21 ! 000000  0    22 " 000000  0   23 # 000000  0
   24 $ 000000  0    25 % 000000  0    26 & 000000  0   27 ' 000000  0
   28 ( 000000  0    29 ) 000000  0    2A * 000000  0   2B + 000000  0
   2C , 000000  0    2D - 000000  0    2E . 000000  0   2F / 000000  0
   30 0 000000  0    31 1 000000  0    32 2 000000  0   33 3 000000  0
   34 4 000000  0    35 5 000000  0    36 6 000000  0   37 7 000000  0
   38 8 000000  0    39 9 000000  0    3A : 000000  0   3B ; 000000  0
   3C < 000000  0    3D = 000000  0    3E > 000000  0   3F ? 000000  0

 WD=decimal widths in 1/120 inch.  TRANSL=hex translation bytes as follows:
    00-7F = output bytes, 80-C5 = tokens, FF = output next byte as is
 PGUP/PGDN = save this screen in memory and go to previous/next screen
        F10  = save this screen in memory and exit    ESC = exit
```

Figure 8-10. Character Translations and Widths from a PAT

Once you've selected the PAT you wish to edit, a selection menu will appear, asking which portion of the PAT you wish to work on. Most of the headings refer to the mechanical movement of your printer and are self-descriptive. Unless you're having problems with things like backspacing or vertical advance, you should leave these settings as they are. The most commonly modified areas are as follows:

Print Styles and Enhancements. Use this to take advantage of print attributes that are available from your printer but not accessed through the PAT. For example, if your printer has the ability to handle condensed type, but the PAT has ignored the function, you can add it here.

Font Descriptors. These are useful for downloading soft fonts or for creating descriptions of fonts for laser printers, such as cartridges used with the Hewlett-Packard LaserJets.

Character Translations and Widths. If your printer is translating a character incorrectly or is giving the character the wrong width, you can modify the PAT here.

User Definable Tokens. This allows you to add extra codes to the PAT. It's useful when special sequences are required, such as initializing the printer before downloading fonts, or sending codes not included in the PAT.

You edit the PAT by calling up the table onscreen. The codes currently in place will be given in either decimal or hexadecimal. (You can switch between the two *by* using the F2 key.) To edit any part of the PAT, you must know the correct code to insert for your printer. This information will come from the printer's documentation. Read the printer documentation carefully and then either modify or add the codes where appropriate.

```
EDIT PRINTER ACTION TABLE           TTYCRLF          User-Definable Tokens I
      F2 will change input mode to ASCII
                                                        o

              BC  ..............       C1  ..............


              BD  ..............       C2  ..............


              BE  ..............       C3  ..............


              BF  ..............       C4  ..............


              C0  ..............       C5  ..............




F10 = save this screen in memory                          ESC to PAT menu
```

Figure 8-11. Example of a Typical PAT

Note: For less-advanced users, the terms decimal, hexadecimal, code, and so forth may seem like technical gibberish. Since it's beyond the scope of this book to explain the workings of computer communications, you should obtain a basic guide to computer/printer operations if these terms are unfamiliar.

To edit the PAT:

• Use the arrow keys to move to the appropriate lines.
• Type in the modifications.
• Press F10 to save the changes.

Your changes are now the print features of *MultiMate Advantage II*. As with any program, the more familiar you become with its workings, the easier it will be for you to use. *MultiMate Advantage II* has enormous power for printing—it just takes a little experimenting and discovering to tap into it.

Chapter 9
MultiMate Math

MultiMate Advantage II offers the user basic mathematical calculations. While the math portion of the program is not designed to replace a calculator, it does offer the opportunity to handle math as part of word processing. This can be very convenient when creating an invoice or other document that requires the manipulation of numbers.

MultiMate Advantage II offers the following calculations:

- Addition
- Subtraction
- Multiplication
- Division
- Percentages
- Exponential functions

The format for handling all calculations is essentially the same and is easy to use. Here's an example of basic addition:

```
        ▌5
        ▌2
        ▌20
Total   ▌27
```

Note that a small square—a *decimal tab*—appears onscreen before each number to be calculated. Decimal tabs are inserted before numbers to tell *MultiMate Advantage II* that a mathematical calculation may be performed, and they identify the numbers to be calculated. The use of decimal tabs is the key to *MultiMate Advantage II* math.

The type of calculation is determined by the symbol placed *before the number* and *after the decimal tab*. Table 9-1 shows the symbols *MultiMate Advantage II* understands.

Table 9-1. Mathematical Symbols

Symbol	Function
No symbol or +	Addition
− ( )	Subtraction
/ or ÷	Division
* or @	Multiplication
⬆ ⬇	Exponent
%	Percent

Use the following procedure for multiplication:

```
        |10
        |*2
Total   |20
```

While the symbols used for mathematical calculations are common, accessing some of them may be new to some users. For example, the up and down arrows used for exponents are actually the *superscript* and *subscript* indicators. These are found by using Alt-Q for superscript and Alt-W for subscript.

In addition, the division sign (÷) is accessed through the *Alternate Math Keyboard*.

To access the Alternate Math Keyboard:

- Press Alt-K until the word MATH appears in the upper right-hand corner of the screen.
- Now press Ctrl-S. The division symbol will appear onscreen.

Calculating

The procedure for calculating is quite exacting and must be carried out precisely in order for the math function of the program to operate. Here's how to do it:

Vertical Math

Step 1

- On a new format line or the current format line, create a tab where you want a vertical column to be calculated.

Step 2

- Place all the numbers to be calculated under the tab using a decimal tab.
- Do this by placing the cursor before the appropriate tab stop and typing Shift-F4.
- A decimal tab will move immediately under the tab.
- Now type in the number plus the symbol telling *MultiMate* which calculation is desired.

Step 3

- On the line on which you wish the total to appear, place a decimal tab at the appropriate place.
- Place the cursor directly under the decimal tab.
- Press Ctrl-F4. The answer will appear to the right of the last decimal tab.

Figure 9-1. Vertical Calculation Showing Format Line with Tab

Rules for Calculations

MultiMate Advantage II can handle any calculation separately (such as subtraction alone or addition alone) or it can combine any of the various calculations. When calculations are combined, *MultiMate* follows this procedure in determining which calculation to do first.

1st	Exponents
2nd	Percentages
3rd	Division/Multiplication
4th	Subtraction/Addition

Figure 9-2 is an example of a combined calculation.

```
DOCUMENT: math                    ‖PAGE:   1‖LINE:  20‖COL:   1‖        INSERT
1--»----»------»-----»-----»----»------»-----»------»----»-----»-----«
ADDITION      »SUBTRACTION     »MULTIPLICATION    »DIVISION     »PERCENTAGE«
  »    ■4    »  ■8      »      »     ■8    »      »    ■64     »  ■100%«
  »    ■4    »  ■-4     »      »    ■×8    »      »    ■/8     »  ■/20«
  »    ■4    »  ■4      »      »    ■64    »      »    ■8.00   »   ■0.05«
  »   ■12«
  »        «
«  .
COMBINED«
  ■5«
  ■-5«
  ■×5«
  ■/5«
  ■0.00«
«
«
«
«
«
«
                                                                        Alt
```

Figure 9-2. Combined Calculation

For negative numbers, the results will be given using the same format in which they were entered. For example, negative numbers can be entered in the following three formats:

(250)

-250

 250-

If the parentheses format is used for the calculation, the result will appear in parentheses. If there's a combination of formats, *MultiMate* will display the results using the following priorities:

1st	Minus Sign Left
2nd	Minus Sign Right
3rd	Parentheses

If you use commas or currency signs in the calculation portion of the math, these will be repeated in the solution portion.

Decimals

You may use decimals as desired with *MultiMate Advantage II* math. The use of the decimal tab will align the numbers with the decimal sign. Here is a typical decimal alignment:

356.998
  .555
242.

The results of calculations will be expressed in decimals carried out as far as room permits. Where no decimals are specified, the results of a calculation are carried out to a maximum of two decimal places.

Horizontal Math

Thus far we have been speaking of math conducted in the normal vertical or columnar fashion. *MultiMate Advantage II* also provides for *horizontal* math. This can be useful when handling receipts or other documents where the numbers are stretched horizontally across a sheet.

TIP: Unlike spreadsheets, *MultiMate Advantage II* does not extend math calculations horizontally to subsequent screens or pages. For significant mathematical calculations, you should use one of the many excellent spreadsheet programs available on the market. Using horizontal math is similar to calculating in the usual vertical fashion.

For horizontal math, follow these steps precisely:

Step 1

- Create a format line that contains tab stops at each point where you want to enter a number. Here, for example, is a format line with five different tab stops.

1----- — »------»------»------»------»--------------------«

- A number will be inserted at each of the first four tab stops. The result will be placed at the last tab stop.

Step 2

- Enter the numbers to be calculated at each tab stop.
    To enter the numbers:
        Enter a decimal tab.
        Press Shift-F4.
- The numbers can be entered with or without decimals.

Step 3

- Place the calculation symbol before the numbers. Remember that no symbol is needed for addition, but symbols *are* needed for all other calculations.

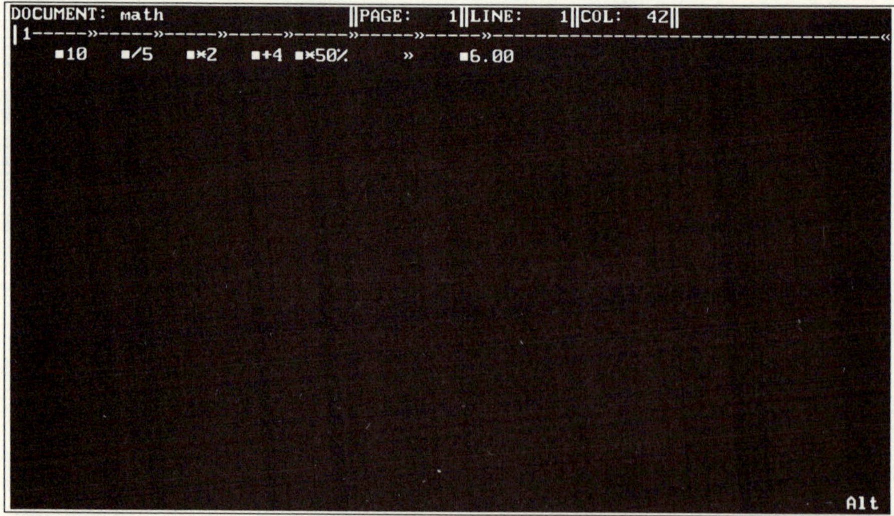

Figure 9-3. Examples of Horizontal Math

Step 4

- After all the numbers have been entered, place a decimal tab at the last tab mark where you want the result to go.
- Place the cursor directly on the decimal tab.
- Press Ctrl-F3.
- The result will appear at the last decimal mark.

TIP: Note that the function keys for vertical and horizontal math are different. Ctrl-F4 is used for vertical math; Ctrl-F3 is used for horizontal math.

As with vertical math, all sorts of calculations using addition, subtraction, exponents, and so forth may be used. Some examples are shown in Figure 9-3.

Exponents

Exponents are expressed using the superscript and subscript arrow symbols, as follows:

- The superscript symbol (Alt-Q) is used to describe the number.
- The subscript symbol (Alt-W) is used to describe the exponent.

For example, 4 squared would be expressed as 4-Alt-Q–2-Alt-W. The result is shown in Figure 9-4.

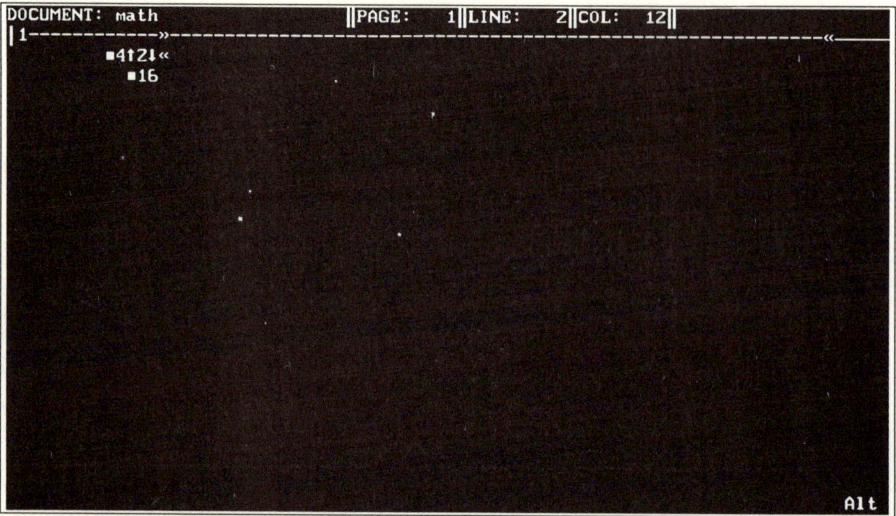

Figure 9-4. Example of an Exponent

The resulting printout would appear as 4". When using exponents in calculations, *MultiMate* does not carry the exponent through to the result. Rather, the result is shown as a whole number.

Columns

MultiMate Advantage II math will work in columns; however, the results may not always be what you anticipate. It's important to remember that columns follow different rules than ordinary text.

Bound Columns. Vertical math does not carry over into succeeding columns.

Snake Columns. Horizontal math does not carry over into succeeding columns.

Chapter 10
Additional Functions

In this chapter, we'll consider three separate advanced functions of *MultiMate Advantage II*: Document Recovery, Boilerplating, and Sorting. Each has a special purpose and useful applications.

Document Recovery

MultiMate Advantage II writes documents to disk as the cursor moves over each page break. In addition, you can command a disk write by pressing Alt-F10. While these procedures should guarantee that what you've written has been saved to permanent memory, this is not always the case.

A glitch in the program, power source, or in some other area can result in an imperfect save, or the program may crash. (The program's publisher suggests that this doesn't happen, but as frequent users know, it can indeed occur.)

Whatever the reason, you may find that part of a file has been lost or damaged, and if that happens, *MultiMate Advantage II* provides an easy-to-use recovery utility. It's important to understand, however, that in order to get the best results, *the recovery must occur before you do any additional editing*. If you do edit after the error, you may inhibit or prevent the recovery of lost data. The recovery program searches the disk for data clusters relevant to the document. If you edit after an error and before recovery— even if you edit a different file—you may write over some of the clusters and make them unrecoverable. So if you detect an error, use the recovery program immediately.

> **TIP:** Errors are usually detected when a file is recalled; however, the error may be at the very end of the file and you may not realize there's a problem until you get to the file end. A good practice is to immediately go to the end of a file as soon as it is reopened. If there's an error, you'll get a message to that effect on the screen.

To recover a document or a portion of a document:

- Select Utility Programs from the opening menu.
- Select Document Recovery from the Utility menu. A new screen will appear, asking for the document file name.
- Give the full directory and path. A list of documents in that directory will appear, one of which will be highlighted.
- Use the space bar to move the highlighting to the file you want to recover.
- Press the F10 key.

MultiMate Advantage II will attempt to recover the file. If it's successful (or partially successful), a message stating that recovery was accomplished will appear onscreen. If it wasn't successful, a message to that effect will also appear.

TIP: If the recovery was unsuccessful, you should try again—a second attempt may succeed. If the recovery is still unsuccessful, exit *MultiMate Advantage II* before doing any other editing, and then use an external utility—such as Norton Utilities—to attempt recovery of the document. Esc will cancel the recovery program and return you to the main menus.

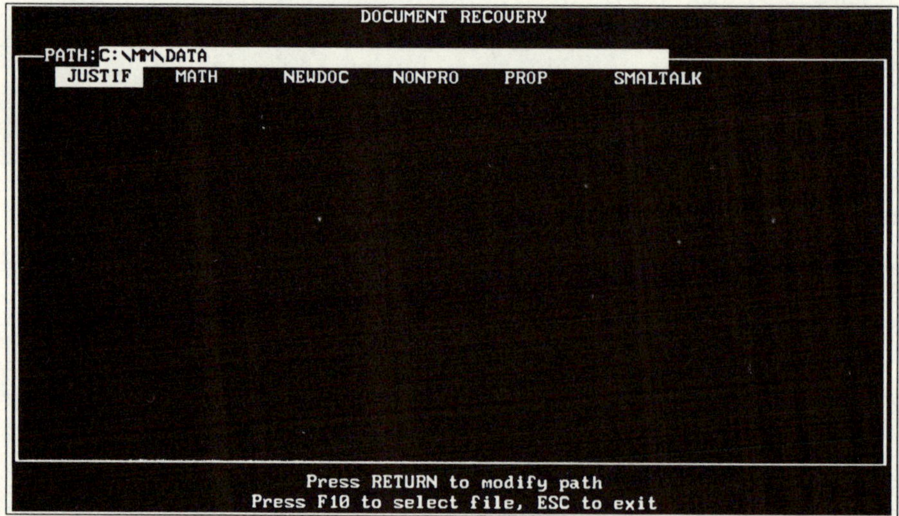

Figure 10-1. Document Recovery Screen

Boilerplating (Library)

In various types of editing—primarily in legal work—there's often the need to create prewritten paragraphs or portions of documents.

As an example, if you're a realtor writing a lease, since many paragraphs are standard and are found in most leases, it would be a waste of time to write a document from scratch every time you needed to produce a lease. It would make far more sense to be able to generate new names and addresses and then have a file of clauses. You could go to the clause you wanted, insert information into the lease, and by repeating the process, create a completed document in a very short time.

This is called *boilerplating*. The paragraphs or files that are kept ready and inserted when needed are called *boilerplate*. In *MultiMate Advantage II,* boilerplating is called a *library* and the files are called *library entries*. (See also the chapters on file merging and macros for more information on boilerplating.)

You can create a variety of libraries, each having many files —a lease library, a dental library, a writing library, and so forth. Each library also contains boilerplate material for you to add to any document you're working on.

To create a library:

- Select Create a New Document from the main menu.
- Type in the library's name (use any descriptive name) and give the full path and directory.
- When the document summary screen appears, do not enter any information; instead, press the F5 key to take you to the library entry screen.

You'll now be asked to make an entry in the library. This is like adding a book to the library or adding a piece to the boilerplating. You may make as many entries as you like, but you're limited to only three characters when naming an entry, so try to make the name as descriptive as possible. (Some users have found that numbers work best as entries; that way you can keep a list of the numbers with a description of what's in the files for later recall.)

Unlike other DOS operations, the library naming system recognizes the difference between uppercase and lowercase.

To activate the file after naming the entry:

• Press the F10 key.

You've now created a library with one entry. You may make as many library entries as you like. Simply repeat the process described above or open the library file as described later in this chapter. You should only make entries that are related, however; in a real estate lease library, for example, you should only enter lease or other contract clauses. In a cookbook library, you would probably only enter recipes. Related entries avoid confusion when it's time to recall the entries.

Using the Library Boilerplating

The purpose of a library is to be able to use it in a document. You want to be able to recall the entry from the library and insert it in text.

To recall an entry from a library:

• The library must be attached to the current document file.
• You must tell *MultiMate Advantage II* which entry to recall and where to place it.
• Open a document file and attach the library.
• Press Shift-F5. A Document Entry screen will appear.
• Give the library name, directory, and path location.

Figure 10-2. Library Entry Screen

One of the more common problems at this point is recalling exactly where the library is located. F6 will display the files in the active drive and directory. If the library is not located there, type in a different directory and press F6 again. In this manner you can search until you find the correct directory.

Once you've attached the library (indicated by a message onscreen), you must tell *MultiMate Advantage II* which entry you want placed into the file and where in the file you want it.

- Place the cursor at the *beginning* of where you want to place the entry.
- Press the F5 key. (This will work only after you've attached the library to the current file.)

MultiMate Advantage II will ask for the entry name. This is the three-character name you previously assigned the entry.

- Press F6 to search the library for existing names if you forget the entry name.
- Press F10 to add the entry to the document.

The entry will now appear onscreen where the cursor was located, and will continue into the document. It may be edited, copied, or otherwise treated like any other text. If you decide you don't want the entry, you can easily erase it.

Creating an Entry from Within a File

Often, it's easier to create an entry for a library *within* a file than to do so separately, as we've done before.

For example, if you're typing a paragraph and realize that it's perfect for boilerplating, you can save it to a library entry.

To create a library entry from within a file:

- Attach a library. If you don't have a library, exit the file and create one as described previously.
- Press Alt-J to mark the text to be copied to the library.
- Create a highlighted block of text in the normal fashion.
- Press F10. When you press F10 to begin the copy, *MultiMate Advantage II* will ask you for an entry name.
- Give a three-character name and press F10 again.
  A library can be edited the same as any other document.

To edit a library:

- Give the library name when you're asked what document to edit. The first entry you made in the library will appear onscreen.
- Use F1 to move to a different entry. (You have to give the correct name to call up an entry.)

You can add to an existing library, but only from the end.

To get to the end:

- Press F1-End.
- Move the cursor to the end of the file and press F2.

The entry screen will appear and you can add a new entry to the file. (For additional information on boilerplating, see Chapter 7, "Merging Files.")

Sorting

It's extremely useful to be able to sort when you're creating a list. *Sorting* allows you to alphabetize quickly and efficiently. *MultiMate Advantage II* allows several different types of sorting, which include the following:

- Sorting by first words
- Sorting by last words
- Sorting by line
- Sorting by blocks of text

Basic Sorting

To begin sorting:

- Determine the text you wish to sort—a list of names, phone numbers, addresses, or any combination.
- Each entry *should be on its own line.*
- Define the list for *MultiMate Advantage II.* To do this, you must move into the column mode.
    Press Shift-F3.
    Select F5, the sort option.
- You now must define the area to be sorted. Use the arrow keys.

Note: You must use the right and left arrow keys before using the down arrow key. Once you use the down arrow key, the left and right arrow keys will be inoperative.

- Press F5 when you are finished.

Sort by First Words

Sorting by first words is useful for most lists. If you want the entry sorted, *MultiMate Advantage II* will begin with the first letter of the first word and alphabetize it against the first letter of the first word of the other entries. For duplicate entries, sorting takes place by second letter, and so forth.

To sort by first words:

- After highlighting and pressing F5, press F10.
- Assuming you want to sort in ascending order (*A* to *Z*), make no changes on the Sort screen that appears.

Sort by Last Words

Sorting by last words is usually the case when you want to sort by state or by individuals' last names. The trick to remember is that the *last word* on the line will be sorted regardless if it's the word you want. You may want to edit the document to be sure all last words are the ones you want sorted before beginning the procedure.

To sort by last words:

- After highlighting the text to be sorted, press F5.
- Press Alt-1. This moves the highlighting on the sort menu to Last Word.
- Assuming you want ascending order (*A* to *Z*), press F10.

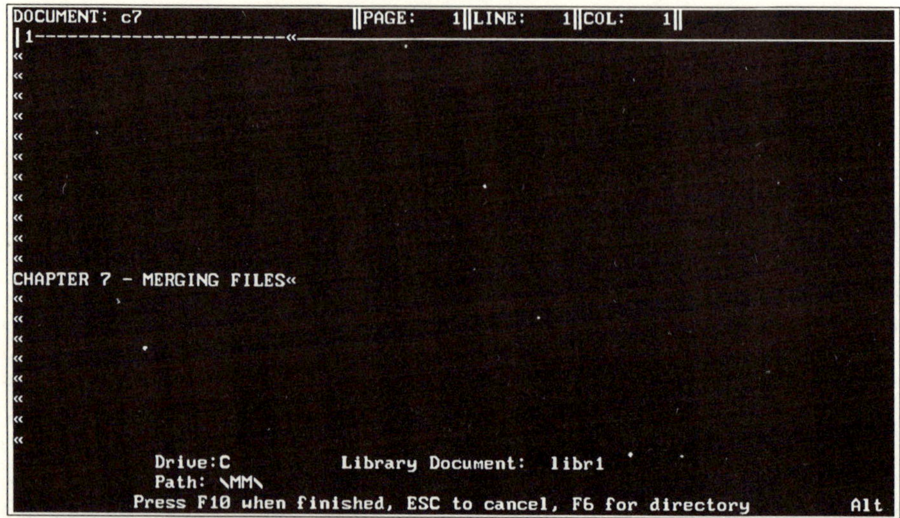

Figure 10-3. Creating a Library

Sort by Sections

It isn't necessary to sort an entire line entry; rather, only a portion of an entry line can be sorted if desired. For example, if you have a list similar to the following,

Name	Address	Route
John Smith	234 Maple	1
Jane Jones	18 Doolittle	2
Art Miller	Route 3, Box 21	3
Henry Johnns	3225 Main St.	4

you want the order of routes to remain the same, but you want the names alphabetized so that individuals are placed in routes by ascending order.

To sort the list by section:

- Highlight only the first two columns.
- Press F5.
- Press Alt-3, Defined Text Only.
- Press F10.

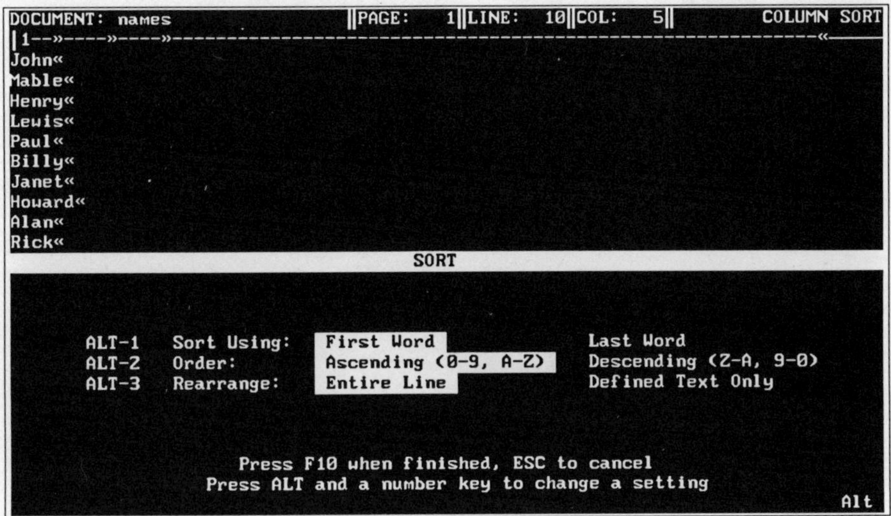

Figure 10-4. Sort Menu

The result will look like this:

Name	Address	Route
Art Miller	Route 3, Box 21	1
Henry Johnns	3225 Main St.	2
Jane Jones	18 Doolittle	3
John Smith	234 Maple	4

Sorting can also be used with numbers such as addresses and phone numbers. Entries are sorted in *ascending* fashion when the numbers are sorted 1–10, and in *descending* fashion when they're sorted 10–1.

Sorting by Line

MultiMate Advantage II sorts by line automatically unless you press Alt-3 in the Sort menu.

Chapter 11

Converting Files

In today's world, with a proliferation of different word processing programs (and word processing as part of spreadsheets and database programs), it's essential to be able to convert files from one program to another. For example, although you may be using *MultiMate Advantage II*, you may need to read files from *WordPerfect, WordStar,* or some other program. Since these files aren't all written in the same format, it's necessary to convert them first.

MultiMate Advantage II provides a utility that will convert files of the most popular programs into *MultiMate*, and in some cases, will convert *MultiMate Advantage II*'s files into formats readable by other programs. The conversion process isn't difficult, but it can be tricky.

Program Conversions

MultiMate Advantage II will convert files for the following formats:

Spreadsheets

123   *Lotus 1-2-3* WKS files can be converted to *MultiMate Advantage II*; *MultiMate Advantage II* files cannot be converted to *Lotus.*

VCDIF   *VisiCalc* .DIF files can be converted to *MultiMate Advantage II*; *MultiMate Advantage II* files cannot be converted to *VisiCalc.*

DIF   Other spreadsheet files that use the .DIF format can be converted to *MultiMate Advantage II*, but not the other way round.

Word Processors

MultiMate Advantage II   This conversion works both ways for *MultiMate Advantage II* into earlier versions of *MultiMate.*

DCA   Document Content Architecture files such as those used by some IBM word processors; conversion works both ways.

WPS   Wang dedicated word processing program; conversion works both ways.

HON   Document from Honeywell word processing; conversion works both ways.

GSA   General Services Administration format; conversion works both ways.

JW   *Just Write;* conversion works both ways.

WST   *WordStar* (old versions, not the new 2000); use the DCA format for *WordStar* 2000; conversion works both ways.

Other Formats

ASCII   This is standard computer code which can be read by almost any MS-DOS program; conversion works both ways.

COMM   A format frequently used for telecommunications.

Conversion Procedure

To convert a program, select the Conversion option from the Utilities menu. You'll have a choice of *converting* or *editing* the conversion parameters; choose Converting.

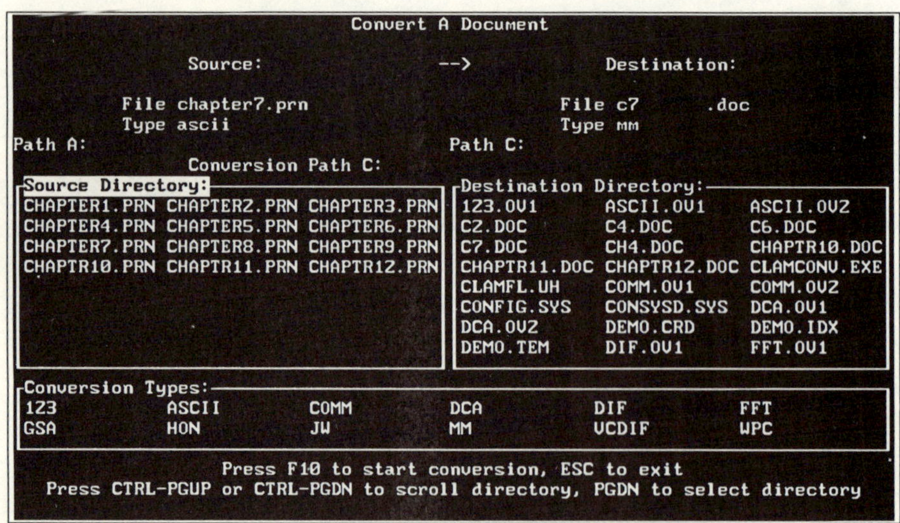

Figure 11-1. Convert a Document Screen

The Convert a Document screen will ask you to specify the file to be transferred, the type of file, and the full directory and path.

File Selected:

• Type in the name of the file you want converted. If you're going from *MultiMate Advantage II* to another format, be sure you give the full *MultiMate Advantage II* filename, such as CHAPTER1.DOC.

File Destination:

• Create a name for the file you want to receive as the result of the conversion. Be sure to type the full name, including the extension.

Directory:

• Type in the source directory of the file to be converted as well as the destination of the file to be created. Be sure to give the drive and full path.
• Press F10. The conversion takes some time so don't expect an instant result.

What Happens in File Conversion

When a file from one format is converted to another format, *MultiMate Advantage II* attempts to replace all the features from the first with corresponding features in the second. Unfortunately, the formats are often not 100 percent compatible, and as a result, conversions usually aren't completely successful.

This isn't to say that the words themselves won't be transferred (almost certainly they will), but the formatting—headers or footers, or most commonly, tabs—won't transfer correctly and the created document may not look exactly like the original.

TIPS: The following are tips for converting files to and from *MultiMate Advantage II.*

- Make the file as simple as possible when going from *MultiMate Advantage II* to another format.
- Avoid the use of tabs unless absolutely necessary. (This is particularly the case going to DCA and *Just Write,* which can't easily handle *MultiMate Advantage II*'s decimal tabs, and from *WordStar,* where tabs are sometimes inserted at spaces and special phantom characters are used.)
- Some word processors either don't have double underlining or they handle boldfacing differently from *MultiMate Advantage II.* Experimentation will quickly disclose the differences.
- *MultiMate Advantage II*'s procedure for handling headers and footers is unique. In some cases it can't effectively be carried over to other formats. In the old version of *WordStar,* for example, only single-line headers and footers are allowed. *MultiMate Advantage II*'s headers and footers can be several lines long. In the conversion, some of the text may be lost; similarly, when converting to Wang, only the first few headers and footers may be converted and the remainder eliminated.
- There are going to be other eccentricities as well, so it's a good idea when converting to examine both the original and the converted files for differences, although most differences will be minor. You may want to modify the original file or even the resulting file if major differences occur.

Special Considerations When Converting to ASCII

ASCII conversion is probably the most common since ASCII files can be read by almost any program, including *MultiMate Advantage II.*

Converting to ASCII

The easiest—and often the best way—to convert a *MultiMate Advantage II* file to ASCII code is to print the document to an ASCII file, rather than use the conversion program. This is handled as part of the printing procedure and is discussed in detail there.

Briefly, the process involves selecting File when you're asked for the destination on the Print Option Screen. You can then write a filename and the file will be "printed" to a new file in ASCII and given a .PRN extension. This ASCII file can then be read directly by most other word processors and can be used for sending the file via modem.

> **TIP:** To configure the resultant file so it can accept the *MultiMate Advantage II* document in ASCII without significant problems, be sure not to set a left margin—*ASCII files cannot handle left margins*. Also, use the Draft print mode and the TTYCRLF PAT. When using the "print file" method, all the print features—including headers, footers, footnotes, print attributes (bold, underline, and so on)—will also be converted; however, the file may not transfer exactly as you want. If you have conversion problems, you can use the Conversion process and adjust the parameters of the transfer.

Editing Parameters When Converting to ASCII

To edit parameters:

- Select Editing Defaults from the File Conversion menu. This will bring up the Edit ASCII Defaults screen.

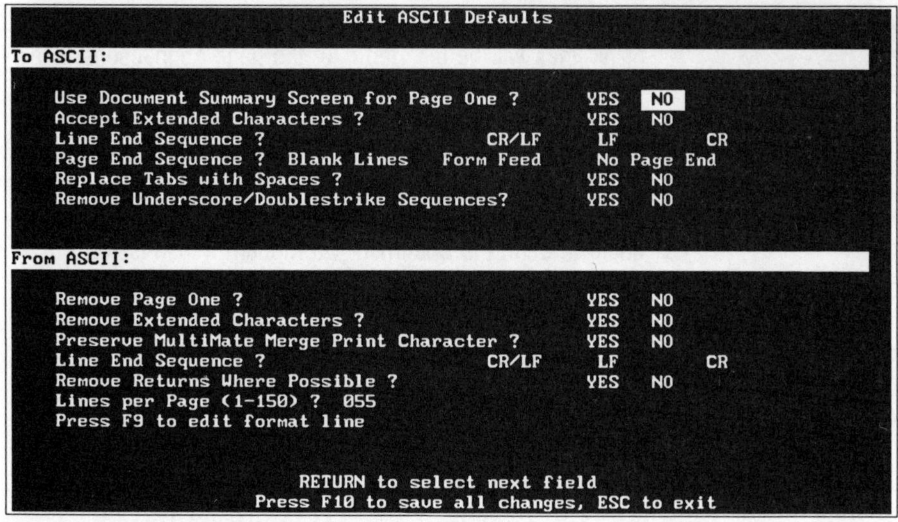

Figure 11-2. Edit ASCII Defaults Screen

Note: This screen is available primarily for editing ASCII conversions. It will not be available for most other conversions.

There are six parameters you may change when converting to an ASCII file.

Document Summary Screen? You can choose whether or not to have the Document Summary Screen included in the transfer. If you choose *Yes,* it will become page 1 of the new file.

Extended Characters? Extended characters are those that don't normally appear on the keyboard. As discussed in the chapter on printing, these may be entered into a file using ASCII decimal code. Choose *Yes* to include these in the converted file; choose *No* to leave them out.

Line End Sequence? One of the problems converting to ASCII is how to handle the end of a line. Normally, both a carriage return (CF) and a line feed (LF) are entered. The problem is if you then use the ASCII file for modem transmission, the file being received will most likely show each line treated as a separate paragraph and thus produce significant confusion.

The answer here will depend on your use of the ASCII file. If it's going to be read by another word processor, you may want to opt for the default (both CR and LF); if you're going to use it for modem transmission, you may want to opt for LF only.

Page End Sequence? ASCII is indifferent when it comes to dealing with the ends of pages—it will handle page ends exactly as you tell it to, offering three options:

Blank Lines	This is useful if you're using continuous-feed paper. The blank lines will be inserted over the page connections, allowing continuous printing at a later time.
Form Feeds	This assumes that each page (when printed) is separately fed into the printer. Each page is ejected after it's written.
No Page End	No page endings; instead, the document is run together as one very long page. This option should be used when you're going to send the document via modem transmission.

Tabs for Spaces? *MultiMate Advantage II* tab characters can be confusing when read by other word processors; therefore, with this option, you can replace *MultiMate Advantage II*'s tabs with spaces. Later on, these spaces can be converted to tabs using the other word processor's editing capabilities.

Underlining? *MultiMate Advantage II*'s underlining capabilities, including double underline, are not converted easily and can produce problems when the resultant ASCII file is read by another program. In most cases, therefore, you should turn your underlining off.

Editing Parameters When Converting from ASCII

MultiMate Advantage II can read some ASCII files directly without any special conversion, although the formatting may be in disarray. This conversion program helps set up the formatting so the resultant file looks more like a *MultiMate Advantage II* file.

As when converting to ASCII, *MultiMate Advantage II* allows you to set six different parameters when converting *from* ASCII. You can reach the main conversion menu by selecting Editing Defaults.

Remove First Page? You'll want to ignore this option unless the ASCII file you're converting has a document description page or something similar. Many word processing programs are now including such a page in the fronts of their files.

Remove Extended Characters? Normal ASCII code is decimal 33–127: Below 33, the code refers to printer and other functions; above 127 refers to extended characters—those using the MSB (Most Significant Bit) or eighth bit of ASCII.

Sometimes the higher-bit ASCII codes are included in the document in the form of special characters. Normally, these characters are converted and included in your *MultiMate Advantage II* file. If you want them eliminated, answer *Yes* here; they'll be replaced by periods in the file.

End Line Sequence? This is useful when receiving ASCII via modem transmission. Depending on how the file was transmitted, you may want to have either line feed (LF) or carriage return (CR) or both.

TIP: If you're not sure which End Line sequence to choose, select LF/CR (both) and see how the file looks onscreen. If each line is a separate paragraph, select one of the other options and reconvert. (LF is most likely to work in this circumstance.)

Remove Returns? The ASCII code may contain lines of various lengths; when converted to *MultiMate Advantage II*, these various line lengths may confuse *MultiMate Advantage II*'s automatic wordwrap. To avoid the confusion, *MultiMate*'s conversion utility will automatically remove extra carriage returns and insert new format lines where necessary. If you want this automatic feature turned off, select *No* here. Beware, though—you may end up with short lines treated as separate paragraphs.

Lines Per Page? You can set the number of lines per page. The default is the standard 55 lines.

TIP: This feature will not reset the lines per page length in the original ASCII document; rather, it's most useful in setting up line length where the ASCII document is all one long page, as may often be the case in modem transmission. When the ASCII document already has page length set, *MultiMate Advantage II* will insert a new page both *whenever it encounters a form feed in the document* and *when it reaches the maximum length set here.* Therefore, unless you want odd-sized pages, set this length longer than the line per page length set in the document (unless the document really has no line per page measure).

Edit Format Lines? This option allows you to set up the format for the resultant document in the ASCII conversion. It's particularly useful for arranging *double spacing, tabs,* and *line length.*

Note: The line length default is set at 156 characters per line. You may want to adjust this down to the more normal 65 to 75 characters per line; 156 is the maximum and can't be adjusted higher.

```
                        Edit Format Line
From ASCII:


|1.............»...............................................................




        Cursor at Column:  27              Right Margin: 156


                       Single Line Spacing




        INS to extend format line  DEL to compress format line
          TAB to insert tab stop  SPACEBAR to remove tab stop
        Use Left and Right Arrows to move within the format line


             Press F10 to save all changes, ESC to exit
```

Figure 11-3. Edit Format Line Screen

Converting To and From Unavailable Formats

Occasionally, you may find that you want to convert to *MultiMate Advantage II* from a word processor that isn't included in the list of possible conversions. For example, you may want to convert to *VolksWriter* or *WordPerfect* (or convert one of those files to *MultiMate Advantage II*).

Converting *From* Nonincluded Word Processors

You can't convert these files directly in most cases; rather, they must first be prepared for you by using the outside word processor's own conversion capabilities.

Have the file from the outside word processor converted to one of the formats that can be read by *MultiMate Advantage II*. For example, in almost all cases, you can have the outside word processor converted to ASCII by having the file printed to disk. In the case of *WordStar 2000*, you can have the file converted to DCA format. Once the outside word processor file has been converted to a format readable by *MultiMate Advantage II*, proceed with the standard conversion process just described.

Converting *To* Nonincluded Word Processors

Other word processors won't (in most cases) be able to read a standard *MultiMate Advantage II* .DOC file; the file must be converted to a format the word processor can read. The two most common formats to use are ASCII and DCA. You'll have to check the documentation of the outside word processor to see exactly which of the two formats will work.

The procedure is to convert *MultiMate Advantage II* .DOC files into a format the other word processor can use; then have the outside word processor either read the file directly or further convert it into its own format. A word of caution, however: Each time a file is converted, some of the original formatting tends to be lost; double conversions, therefore, sometimes produce unexpected and unwanted results.

Note: When dealing with spreadsheets, MultiMate Advantage II *can't be converted to the other formats—only to* MultiMate Advantage II.

Preparing a Document for Modem Transfer

Although we've covered this in various places, those who wish to prepare a document for modem transmission may find the following information helpful.

MultiMate to *MultiMate*

MultiMate Advantage II provides a special COMM format for modem transmission. This is particularly useful if both the sender and receiver are using *MultiMate Advantage II*. If both are not, certain concerns may arise.

For example, earlier versions of *MultiMate Advantage II* didn't have the double underline feature nor the ability to insert extended ASCII characters directly into text. If these are sent using the COMM conversion, they'll confuse the receiving word processor; therefore, they should be deleted from text before transmission.

MultiMate Advantage II to Other Word Processors

While the COMM conversion may allow other word processors to receive *MultiMate Advantage II* files, in most cases, the ASCII conversion noted above should prove more useful. This is also true when sending *MultiMate Advantage II* files that contain footnotes to earlier versions of *MultiMate*. When preparing to send via modem, set the following parameters to help avoid problems later on:

• Do not prepare the document to be sent by using the Print To File option from the Print method. While this may work, it can create problems.

• Use the ASCII conversion file option under the Utilities menu.
• Prepare the file to be transferred:

> If possible, eliminate all tabs. These can be confused in transmission and may produce unexpected results in the resultant file.

> If possible, remove all headers and footers. Instead, type a suggested header and footer at the top of page 1 (not using the Alt-H or Alt-F commands) so the person receiving the file can later create headers and footers using the facilities of the receiving word processor.

> Place all footnotes at the end of the document. This will avoid confusing footnotes for text in the transmission. If properly numbered, the receiving user can easily convert them to footnotes using the receiving word processor.

> Avoid using the carriage return in the file except for ending paragraphs.

Setting Parameters

Set the parameters for the file transfer (select Edit Conversion from the Conversion menu) to the following:
Note: These are suggestions; experiment to see if they work for you. If not, you may want to set your parameters differently.

Document Summary Screen? Set to *Off;* otherwise, the Document Summary screen will appear as the first page of text and will be confusing. If it's necessary to send the document summary screen, send it as the first page of a separate file.

Extended Characters? Set to *On* or *Off,* depending on the capabilities of the receiving program.

Line End Sequence? Set to LF for Line Feed. In most cases, this will result in a normal transmission. You may need to adjust the line end sequence, depending on the parameters of the receiving program.

Page End? Set to *No.* For most modem transmission, you don't want to have a page end unless you've already set up the parameters for *page ending* with the receiving program. Therefore, select No Page End.

Replace Tabs With Spaces? Set to *Yes.* Again, unless the receiving program is set up to handle *MultiMate Advantage II* tabs, select *Yes.* The user at the other end can then go back and insert tabs at the appropriate spaces.

Remove Underscore/Doublestrike? Set to *Yes*. Answer yes unless the receiving program is set up to handle *MultiMate Advantage II* underlining and doublestriking.

These parameter settings won't guarantee a perfect transmission the first time, but they should go a long way toward avoiding problems. Keep in mind that modem transmission between different word processors is tricky. Each word processor tends to handle formatting and other editing chores differently, so you may need to experiment some—you may have to send the same file several times before getting a perfect transmission.

Working with Templates

MultiMate Advantage II offers the ability to create "mini" data files for use at home and in the office. You can keep records of customers, or recipes, or even appointments. The data file system is easy to set up; it can be printed using the merge facilities, discussed in an earlier chapter; and it can help keep all sorts of data in order.

Note: This data file *system shouldn't be confused with On-File, a separate companion program to* MultiMate Advantage II, *discussed in the next chapter.*

MultiMate Advantage II refers to the data files as *information handling*. While descriptive, the term really doesn't begin to suggest the power offered to users by this function. In addition, the documentation is somewhat foggy on the use of templates within a data file. Since templates are essential to the operation of *MultiMate Advantage II*'s data file system, in this chapter, we'll refer to them as *template data files*.

How a Template Data File Works

The operation of a template data file is quite simple. On the first page of a special document, you create a *template*—a convenient method of organizing the data you're going to enter into a file. The template can be almost any kind of information you want *repeated* on each page of the file. The simplest template would be as follows:

Name: —
Address: —
City, State: —

This would be recorded on the template (the first page of the file), and would reappear on each subsequent page. You would only have to fill in the information requested by each label (Name, Address, and so on).

The data you enter for each label becomes a *field*. All data entered for all fields on a page becomes a *record*. Later on, you can sort the records (the pages in the document), add to them, search for specific information in them, select them, and even print them.

Creating a Template

To begin creating a template:

• First open a data file. This is a little different from opening a regular file.

> *To open a data file:*
>> Select 2 from Create a File (the opening menu).
>> Fill in the name. Use a name that suggests a *data* rather than *document* file.
>> Press the F10 key.

• To get to the Document Summary Screen (and if desired, fill it out in the normal fashion):

>> Press Shift-F10. Normally, you would press only the F10 key; however, Shift-F10 tells *MultiMate Advantage II* that you want to create a data file. You're immediately taken to page 1, which is the template page.

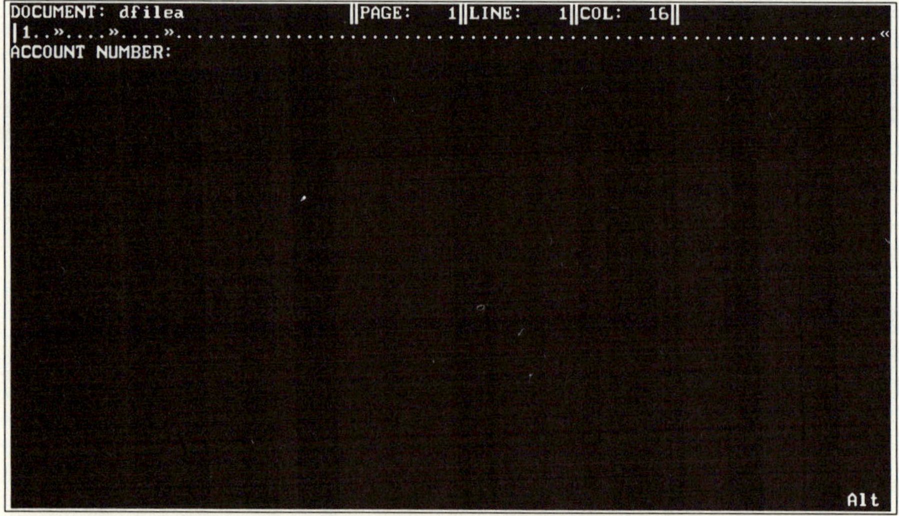

Figure 12-1. Template Page

Creating Labels on a Template Page

A label is an identification word on a template. For example, *Name* on a template would identify the field into which you wish to enter a person's name.

• Type a label *ended by a colon.*

For example, if on the first page you type *Address:,* this becomes a label—it will appear whenever the template is called up. You can't edit or change it directly.

Note: You're limited to labels that are no more than 79 characters long.

After entering a label, you must provide a place for data to be entered. Do this by creating a *field* using the underlining function.

To create a field:

• Type a label (Name:). Be sure to end the label with a colon.
• Add underlining where the field is to go:
> Press Alt-= (to turn on underlining).
> Press Shift-— (to underline).
• The result will be

Name: —

which you'll see on the record pages (the data file pages following the template).

You won't be able to edit the word *Name:,* but you'll be able to add data at the underline, and you'll be able to edit that data.

The amount of data you enter into any one field is limited by the amount of underlining. If the name is longer than the underlined area you've allowed, you simply won't be able to type in the entire name. The maximum length for any single field is 255 characters (which is more than enough for most practical uses). If you exceed 255 characters, you'll get the error message FIELD SIZE EXCEEDS 255 CHARACTERS.

The following is a template created for use in a loan office.

Account Number: –

Husband's Name: –

Wife's Name: –

Property Address: –

City: –
State: – – – – – – ZIP: – – – – – – – – – – – – – – – – – – –

Bdrms: – – – – – – – – Baths: – – – – – – – – Pool: – – – – – – –
Yard: –

Current Financing: – .

Est. Close Date: – – – –/– – – –/– – – – – – – – – – – – – – –

This template was created in just a few minutes, yet it serves the office on a daily basis. The labels were simply typed in with underlining to indicate where the field data was to be entered. Anyone using the file can easily add records or locate information.

Adding Records
Adding records to the data file is quite easy.

To add the first record:
- Create the template.
- Press Ctrl-PgDn.
- Answer *Yes* when asked if you want to leave the template page. This will take you to the first record. You may now begin entering data in the fields.

You can add subsequent records after you've filled out a "record page."

To add subsequent records:

• Press Page Down. This will take you to the end of the current page.
• Press the F2 key. A new record page will appear, complete with the template in place.

Additional functions:

• Use F2 to add a record anywhere in the file.
• Add to the very beginning of the file by going back to the template (to be discussed shortly) and pressing F2.
• Add after any existing record in the file by first going to that record (F1-[Record #]) and then pressing F2.
• Add to the end of the file by first pressing F1 and then End to take you to the last record.

> **TIP:** At the template, press Ctrl-PgDn to go the next record, whether it's blank or filled with data. Pressing F2 at the template page creates a new blank page immediately following the template.

Editing the Template

From the data file, you can't return to the template page or edit it. This is simply to protect you from creating havoc in the file. Changing the template while in the file would mean a possible disruption of fields and records.

To access the template:

• Exit the file.
• Call up the file.

As soon as the file reopens, you'll be in the template page. You may now edit it as you wish, but use the following cautions:

• If you shorten a field on the template when you already have data in that field in various records, you could lose some of your data. *MultiMate Advantage II* will warn you of this with the message SHORTENED FIELD LENGTH MAY CUT OFF DATA.

DO YOU WISH TO CONTINUE (y/n?). In most cases you would opt for *No* and rethink the situation.

- If you delete a label on the template when you already have data in that label's field in various records, you'll lose the data. *MultiMate Advantage II* will warn you of this with ARE YOU SURE YOU WANT THE LABEL DELETED? (y/n).

- The template format line must be 80 characters long—there are no exceptions. If you attempt to alter the length of the format line, an error message will appear: FORMAT LINE MUST BE 80 COLUMNS.

- You can't use column mode in a template. You're restricted to a single column.

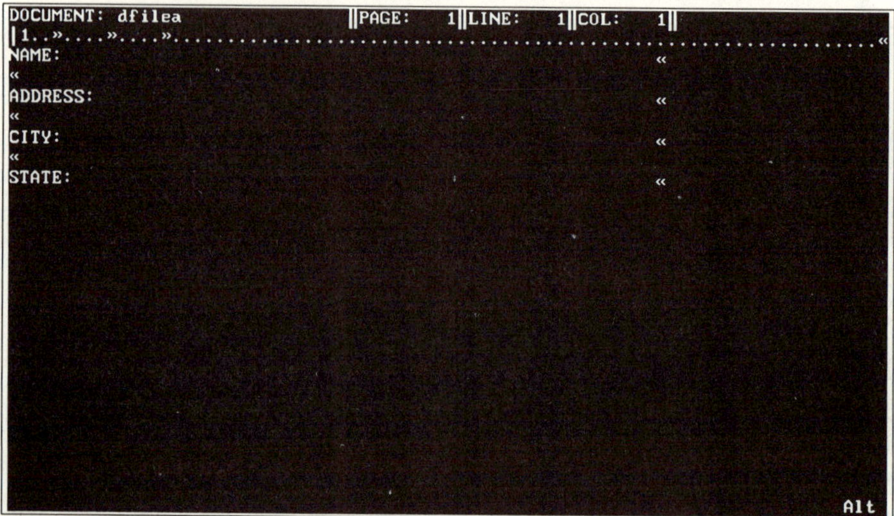

Figure 12-2. Edited Template Page

Data File Management

Once you've created a data file of numerous records (you can have up to 255 separate page records), you may want to sort, search, or even print them. *MultiMate Advantage II* provides facilities to accomplish each of these functions and more.

Moving Through the Record Pages

To move forward record by record:

- Press Ctrl-PgUp

To move backward record by record:

• Press Ctrl-PgDn

Editing Records

When moving forward and backward, you can edit any record. Use the arrow keys as well as PgDn and PgUp to move to different fields and then delete or add data as desired. You may also use the *Search and Replace* function of *MultiMate Advantage II* to change data in a field.

To use the Search and Replace function:

• Place the cursor in the field you want replaced.
• Press Shift-F6 (to activate Search and Replace).
• The Search and Replace screen appears at the bottom of your monitor.
• Type in the data to replace the information in the current field.
• Press F10. The old data will be replaced by the new.

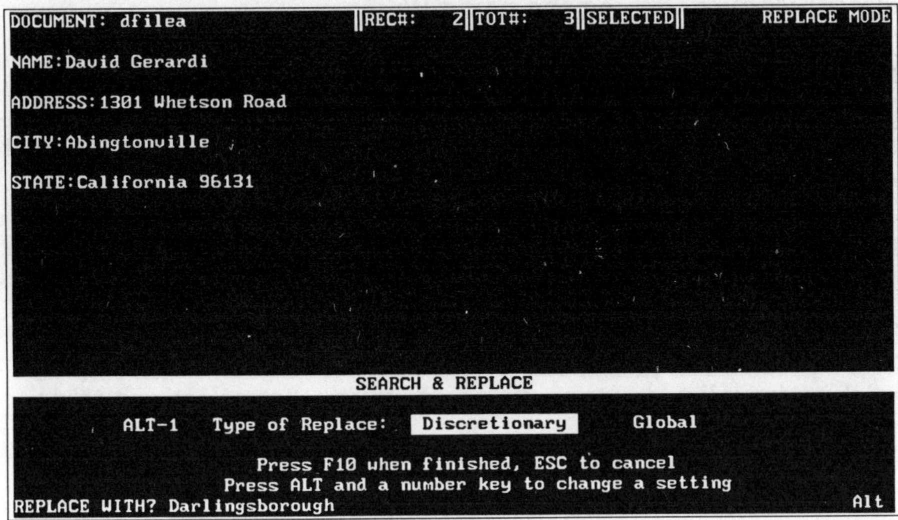

Figure 12-3. Search and Replace Screen

This function is particularly useful when you have a large field. Be careful, however, not to exceed the length of the field with the new data.

Deleting a Record

Any page record in a data file may be deleted. Be sure you're in the record you wish to delete.

To delete a file:

- Press Shift-F2.
- Before deleting the file, *MultiMate Advantage II* will ask if you're sure you want it deleted. Answer *Yes*.

Sorting Records

MultiMate Advantage II will automatically sort the records in the data file in either ascending or descending order. While the procedure is quite simple, it's important to understand that records are sorted only one field at a time. This can produce some unexpected results.

For example, if you begin by sorting the records for a field labeled *Name*, in ascending order, all the names in that field will be sorted. Thus, a record containing the name *Ambrose* will come before a record containing the name *Wilson*.

Suppose after sorting by *Name* you decide to resort according to a label called *City*. If Ambrose lives in Washington and Wilson lives in Albuquerque, the Wilson file will come before the Ambrose file when sorted in ascending order. For proper results, sort carefully.

To sort:

- Be sure the cursor is in the field you want to sort.
- Press the F5 key. Sort mode will be engaged and the Sort Option menu will appear onscreen.
- Select *Ascending* or *Descending* and make other selections as desired.
- Press the F10 key. The entire data file will be sorted according to the field in which the cursor has been placed.

Printing Records

With *MultiMate Advantage II*, you can

- Either print all the records in a data file or print only selected records.
- Print records with or without the template labels.

- Use the data in a data file as a merge list for insertion into a merge document. (See Chapter 7, "Merging Files.")

To print all records without labels:

- Move to the first record in the file, using Ctrl-PgUp.
- Press Alt-F1. The message SELECTED will appear on your screen.

To select the files to be printed:

- Press Alt-F1. This selects the first record.
- Press Alt-Y. This tells *MultiMate Advantage II* that you wish to select additional records.
- A message appears asking if you want to select all the remaining records, cancel, or leave all remaining records unselected:
    Highlight SELECTED.
    Press the F10 key.
- Now print the file; all records will be printed.

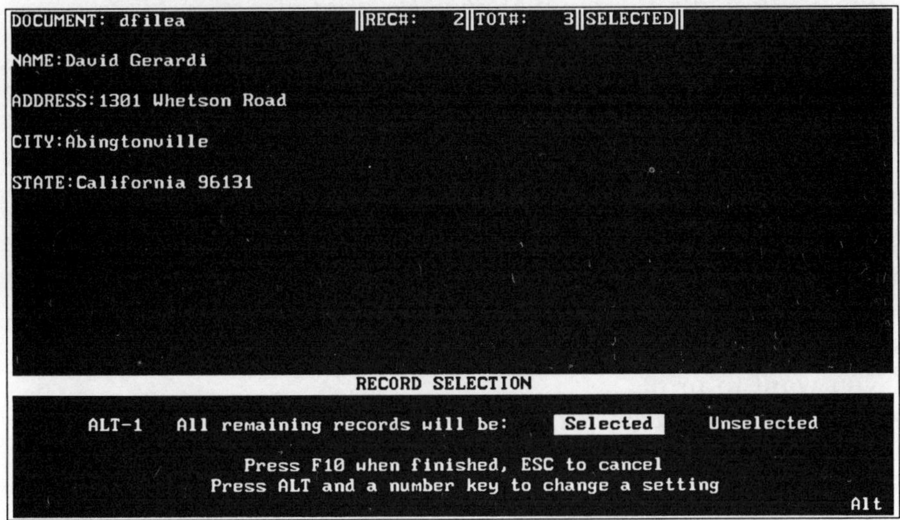

Figure 12-4. Select Message

To print selected records without labels:

- Move through the data file until you reach the first record you want to print.
- Press Alt-F1. That record is selected.

- If you also want to select all following records:
    Press Alt-Y.
    Highlight REMAINING RECORDS.
- If you don't want to print remaining records:
    Highlight UNSELECTED.
    Press F10.
- To select additional records for printing:
    Move to the record.
    Press Alt-F1.

You may want to print a form—the template without any data entered into the fields. This is easily accomplished.

To print the template without data in the fields:

- Do not select any records for printing.
- Select Print from the main menu.
- Give the data file name and complete the Document Print Options screen.
- Press F10. Only the template will be printed.

To print records with the template showing:

- You must use the Merge Print function accessed from the main menu.
- When asked to name the Merge Document, use the name of the data file.
- When asked to name the Merge List (data file), leave the space empty.
- Press F10. A screen will appear, asking for the pages (records) you want to print.
- Select the records to print. (Remember that in most cases each page will be a separate record.)
- Press F10. The Document Options Screen will appear; complete it in the normal fashion.
- Press F10 to print. The records will now be printed showing the labels.

Note: Since you're using the Merge Print function to print the labels as well as the data, you obviously cannot use the data file as a list with labels in another merge procedure—you can't merge print the data with labels into a separate document. Only the field data can be used for merging in a separate document.

Error Messages

When working with the data file, you may occasionally run into an *error message*. Some of these we've covered already; here are a few others that may occur:

LABEL IS A DUPLICATE LABEL. The name you give a label must be unique. For example, you can't have two labels called *Name*. However, you can have two labels called *Name* and *NAME*. *MultiMate Advantage II* recognizes the difference between upper- and lowercase for the purposes of the data file.

You *can* have duplicate names *after the first 12 characters*. For example, you could have two files named 1234567890ABSMITH and BA0987654321SMITH. The name *SMITH* can be identical since it comes after the first 12 characters.

PAGE TOO LARGE, CANNOT EXCEED 66 LINES. The maximum length for a template page is 66 lines.

TEMPLATE HAS NO DATA FIELDS. You have to enter at least one data field.

OLD LABEL NAME MISSING, HAS IT BEEN RENAMED? (y/n). This is a reminder that you've changed a label. If you answer *No,* you may lose all the data for that label. If you answer *Yes,* you'll be asked to give the new label name.

Lines and Boxes

You can use *MultiMate Advantage II*'s line- and box-drawing functions as well as the alternate keyboard graphics functions in conjunction with text to create very eye-appealing and effective templates.

Figure 12-5 is an example using the loan office template shown at the beginning of the chapter.

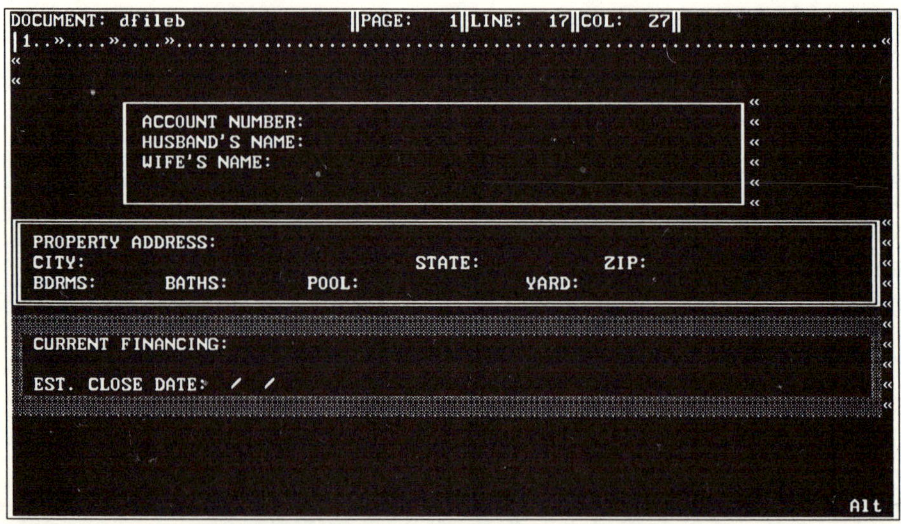

Figure 12-5. Loan Office Template with Lines and Boxes

Adding Default Data

Sometimes it's helpful to have some of a template already filled out. For example, in a doctor's office, one of the labels might be DOCTOR'S NAME, and it would be convenient to have the doctor's name already filled in.

To add default data:

- Create the label (in this case, DOCTOR'S NAME:).
- Remember that the colon ends the label. Normally at this point, you would use underlining to create a field to be filled in at a later time.
- Where the field would normally go, Press Alt-–.
- Type in the doctor's name.
- Press Alt-– again to end the entry.

The label and field will now look like this:

DOCTOR'S NAME: Dr. Bill Smith, M.D.

Later on, when you call up a record, the field for DOCTOR'S NAME will be filled in already. Similarly, when printing, *Bill Smith* will appear just as if it had been separately entered.

MultiMate Advantage II's template is a powerful function that can provide useful service when you're working with a small data file. For longer and more complex data files, you should install a database management program such as dBASE.

Chapter 13
Working with On-File™

On-File is a separate database management program that's normally shipped as a companion to *MultiMate Advantage II*. It's a powerful program that allows you to create an electronic filing system.

On-File is conceptually based on a simple card-file index. The records are called *cards,* the files in which the records are kept are called *card boxes,* and the onscreen graphics depict *boxes of cards.* The program allows you to create numerous card boxes, in which "decks" of cards are kept. You can have a variety of decks and as many as a thousand cards in a each deck. The whole point of the program is to allow you to easily and quickly store large amounts of information and then manipulate that information so you can extract it in whatever form you want.

For example, you might have a file with thousands of phone numbers, addresses, and comments. Once entered, you could sort through the file and extract data based on ZIP codes, area codes, last names, or whatever you want. You can create a file to handle invoices or even recipes—On-File's use is limited only by your imagination.

Note: On-File is similar to the database system incorporated in MultiMate Advantage II, *which has been discussed in previous chapters. However, On-File is much more powerful and flexible. For small database applications, you may want to remain inside* MultiMate Advantage II, *but to create a database of any significant size, you'll want to use On-File.*

Calling Up On-File
You can call up On-File two different ways:

- One way is to select 2 from the opening menu of *MultiMate Advantage II.* You'll be taken to On-File immediately.
- The other way is to be in the drive and directory in which the On-File program resides (normally the same directory as used for *MultiMate Advantage II*); then type *onfile.* The program will appear onscreen.

Understanding the Cards

The first thing to understand about On-File involves the *cards,* which are the basis of the On-File system. As with actual 3 × 5 inch index cards, On-File's cards are merely records into which you add information.

You can create templates to fit over the cards or simply add data in a raw fashion. We'll take a look at the cards in a moment, but first, let's consider what the cards themselves are made up of, which consists of five separate areas.

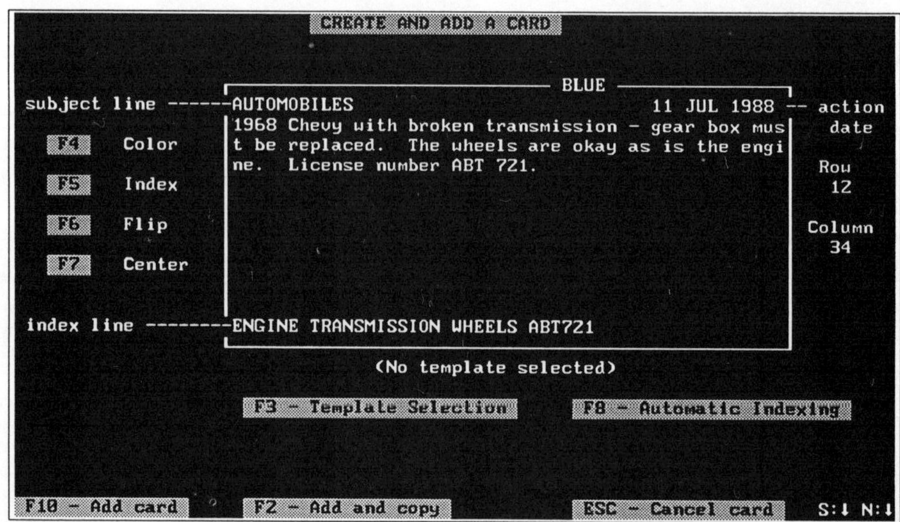

Figure 13-1. Typical Card on the Create and Add a Card Screen

Subject Line. You'll give the subject of the card on this line. For example, in a medical file the card might have a title such as "Diabetics"; in an automotive file it could be "Transmissions." The idea behind the subject line is to identify the basic area of the card. You can put up to 35 characters on the subject line.

Action Date. This gives you a time reference for the card. Normally the action date is automatically entered when you create the card; however, you may change the action date at any time. The Action Date line is limited to 11 characters.

Data. The data is entered either on the front or back of the card (F6 toggles you back and forth between front and back). You can enter up to 10 lines on the front and 12 lines on the back, but you're limited to about 50 characters per line.

Color. Just as with index cards—when you have a set of cards in blue and another in green, and so on—On-File gives you a variety of colors to use to set off some cards from others in the file. (F4 allows you to toggle through the colors.)

If you have a color monitor, the borders of the file card will be displayed in the color chosen. Otherwise, the name of the color will be displayed at the top of the screen. Colors you can choose from include

Blue	Purple
Brown	Red
Green	White
Pink	Yellow

Index Line. This is the bottom line on the front of the card and is reserved for key words from the data in the card. (You can easily transfer key words from the data in the card to the index line.)

The key words in the index line can later be used to sort the card. For example, if you have the key word "Clutch" in a card with the subject of "Transmissions," you can later call up the card by searching for the word *clutch* on the Index line. The Index line is limited to 50 characters.

Getting Started with On-File

Once you have the idea that data can be entered into the file cards, the easiest way to understand how the program works is to use it.

To go to On-File:

- After correctly installing On-File, type 2 from the opening *MultiMate Advantage II* menu.
- Press Enter. This will take you directly to On-File.

    The copyright screen for On-File is the first screen you'll see.

To go past the copyright screen:

- Press the space bar.
- The next screen will be the box selection screen.

```
                    MULTIMATE ON-FILE

                       Version 2.0A

     MultiMate International, An Ashton-Tate Company
     52 Oakland Avenue
     East Hartford, CT  06108-9911   USA


 Available Boxes:

   MLIBRARY      DEMO          NEW







          Drive: C       Box Name:      NEW

          Enter the name of your box and press return
               PgUp/PgDn - Select drive              S:↓ N:↓
```

Figure 13-2. Box Selection Screen

Here you're asked either to give the name of the box of cards you want to open, or to create a new box. If you've never before used On-File, create a new box.

To create a new box:

- Type in a name for the box.
- The name should be descriptive of all the files the box will contain. For example, you might call the box *Legal* if it's going to contain all your legal data.

To access an existing box:

- Type in the correct name.
- Remember that the "box" holds the file cards and is roughly equivalent to a card file box.
- You'll now be taken to the opening menu.

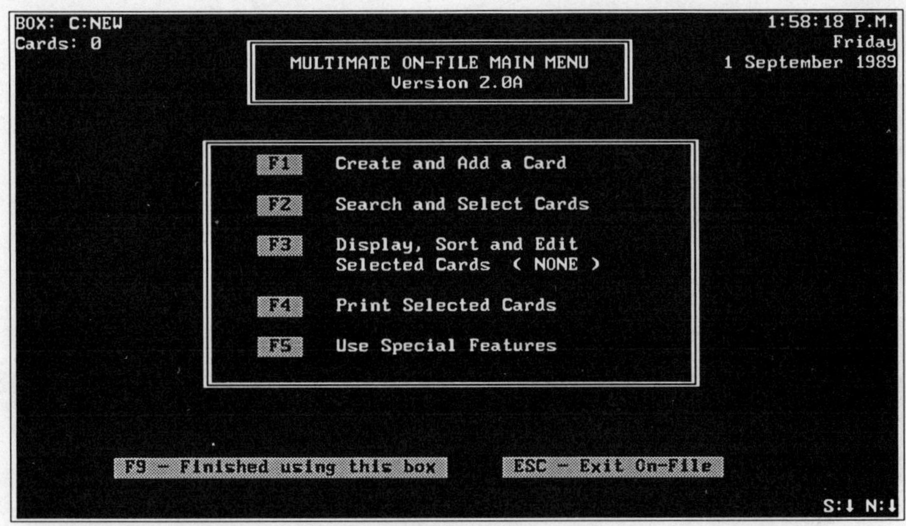

Figure 13-3. On-File Opening (Main) Menu

The opening menu gives you five separate selections:

F1   Create or add a card
F2   Search and select
F3   Display, Sort, Edit
F4   Print
F5   Move to special features.

Creating a Card

To create a card:

- Press F1.
- You'll be taken to the Create and Add a Card Screen. What you see onscreen is the card itself, although it's blank.
- A few basics you should know when entering information on the card:

    Use F7 to center data.

    The date is given in the upper right-hand corner.

    The row and column the cursor is on is given directly below the date.

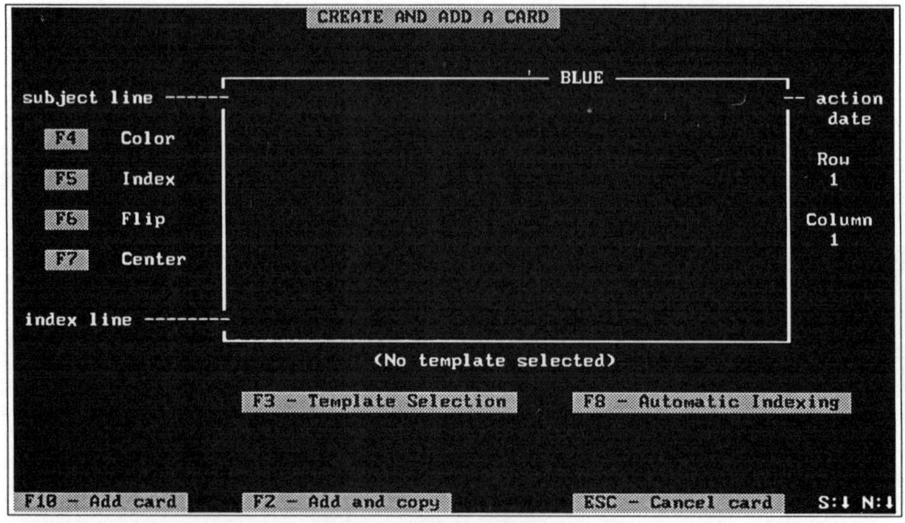

Figure 13-4. Create and Add a Card Screen

Entering Information On a Card

Now, you need to add information. As an example, we'll assume you're working in an auto supply warehouse. Here's how to enter data to a typical card.

Subject Line

The subject of this card is "Holly Carburetors."

• Type in *Holly Carburetors*.

Data Lines

Now type in any data you have on the subject—you may want to list the parts of a Holly Carburetor, or how to assemble or disassemble one, or even note the gaskets that are used.

Remember, you can type up to 10 lines on the front of the card and 12 more on the back. (Use F6 to toggle between the front and back of the card.)

When you've finished entering the data, enter key words on the index line so you can later extract this card from the key words. For example, if your key words for this record are *Assem-*

bly, Parts, and *Gaskets,* you could sort through the box for *Gaskets* and this card would pop up.

There are several methods of entering key words on the index line. The easiest is to take the words right from the text.

To enter words from text on the index line:

- Place the cursor under the first word you want entered in the Index line. In this case, it might be "assembly."
- Press F5. The word will be entered onto the index line.

To use an alternate method of adding words to the index line:

- Go to the index line.
- Press F5.
- Type in the key words.
- The words can be no longer than 18 characters.
- To separate the words, press the space bar. This places a space separating the words.
- On-File will now search through the existing cards in the box and will put key words from those cards onscreen.

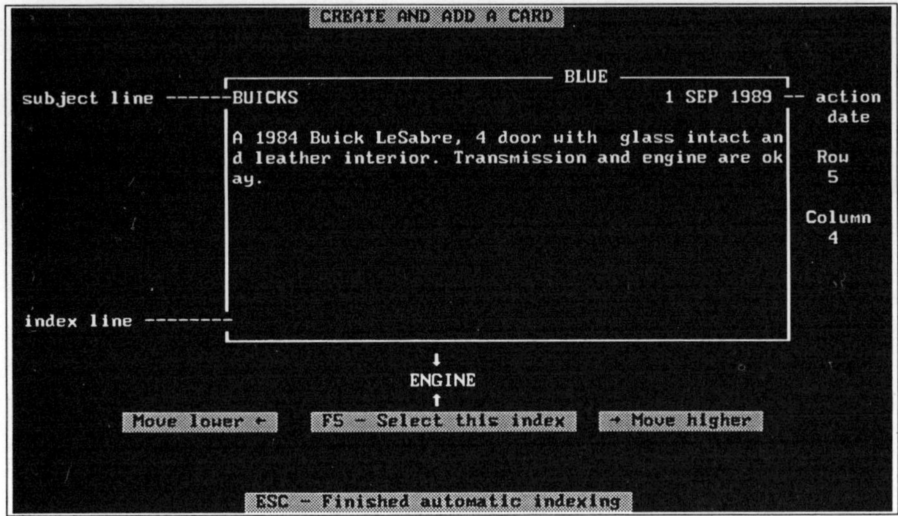

Figure 13-5. Example of Automatic Index Words

You can also enter key words previously entered from other cards. This is called *automatic indexing*.

To engage automatic indexing:
- Press F8.
- Scroll through the list, using the right and left arrow keys.
- Press F5 when you find a word you want from the existing index entered into this index.

Note: You're limited to 50 characters (including spaces) on the index line, so try to index only the key words.

Color

You may change the color of your card.

To change the color:
- Press the F4 key. Pressing F4 repeatedly will alternate the color of the card—for example, if you want all carburetors to be colored red, all transmissions blue, all engines green, and so forth. To get to all carburetor cards quickly, you only need to sort by color.

Once you've finished entering data, you can review the information.

To review the data:
- Press the F2 key.

To add the card to the box:
- Press the F1 key.

To cancel the card:
- Press the F10 key.

Templates

While the information you've just added to the card in your box is easily accessible, it would be even more accessible if you were able to enter the date in a similar fashion in all cards.

For example, if you're working in a dental office using On-File, you could enter every patient's name, diagnosis, and other information in paragraph fashion, but it would be much easier if you had a template with labels that asked for name, address, phone, condition, visits, work done, and so on. The template produces uniform labels that help to put data into a more orderly fashion.

On-File allows you to create many templates within the same box and to switch them around. On one card, a template could be used for entering medical information; on another card, it could be used for entering insurance data, and so forth. You must create the templates beforehand.

To create a template:

- Select F5, the Special Features screen, from the opening menu of On-File.
- Press F3 to go to the Create and Edit Templates screen.
- Press F1. This allows you to create a brand new template.

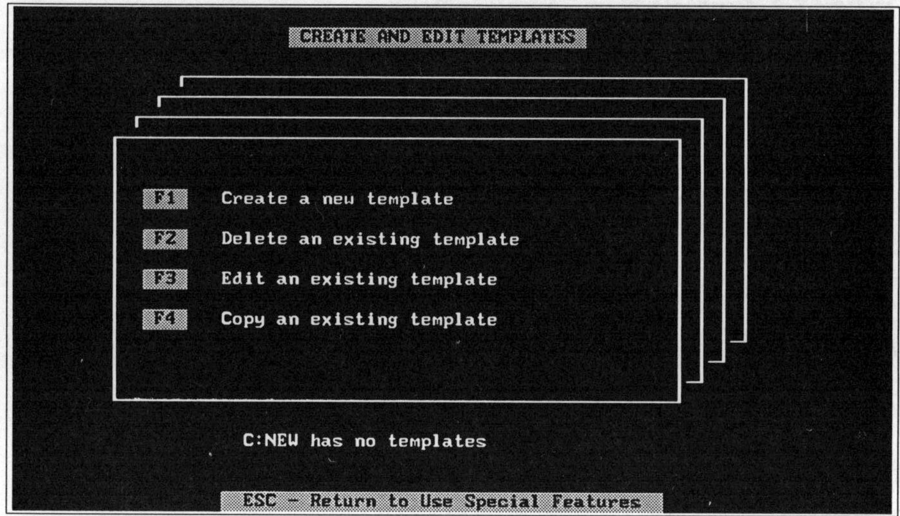

Figure 13-6. Create and Edit Templates Screen

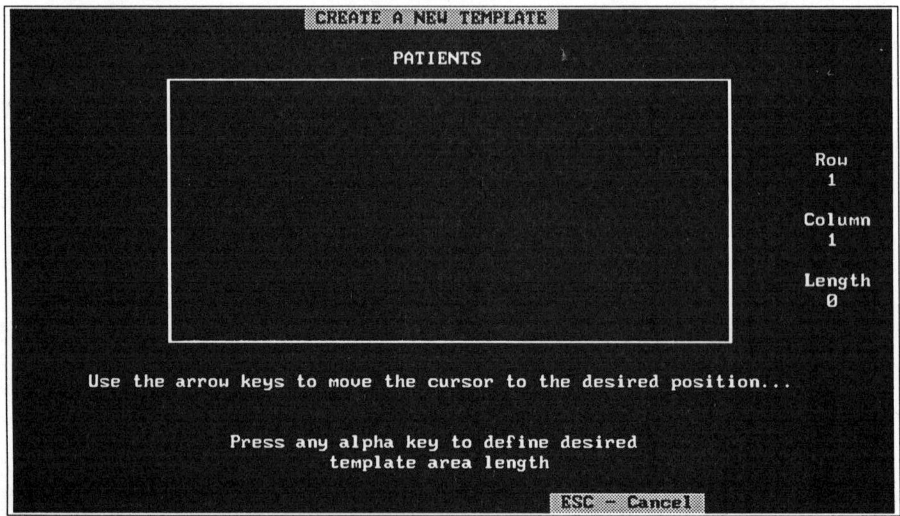

Figure 13-7. Create a New Template Screen

- You'll first be asked to create a name for this template. The name should describe the template's function—for example, *Clients.*
- You'll next be asked to enter the area to be covered by the first field. Move the cursor to the area where you want the field to be.
- Type any letter to enter the length of that field. On-File recognizes the alpha characters (*A–Z*) as spacers. It doesn't matter whether you choose an *A* or a *W* or an *L*—the letters only create a space where the field for the label will be.

To tell *MultiMate Advantage II* that you've indicated the field area:

- Press F10. Now *MultiMate Advantage II* will ask you to give a title to the area. (The word *title* is used in On-File instead of the word *label*.)
- Type in a descriptive title for the field you've just indicated.
- Press Enter. The title will be entered onscreen.
- You may now indicate a new area where you want to create another field. To do so, repeat the process. You may use the entire surface of the card for your fields.
- Press F10. This completes the template.

Figure 13-8. Card Filled Out with Fields, Showing Letter Spacing

Edit an Existing Template

At a later time, you may want to go back and make changes on your template or add a new field area. You can access an already-created template.

To edit the titles of an existing template:

- Press F9 to choose the template.
- Press F3 from the Create and Edit Templates menu.
- You may now edit the titles of a template. Use the arrow keys to move to the area you wish to edit and make the changes.

To add a new area to an existing template:

- Press F1 from the Create and Edit Templates menu.
- Move the cursor to where you want to add the new area. (Either use the arrow keys or press Enter.)
- Define the new area in the same fashion as if you were creating a new card, using the alpha keys as described earlier.
- Press F10.
- Give the area a title (as described earlier).
- Press Enter.

To save your changes:

- Press F10

Resequence a Template

Information added to a card using a template is usually inserted in the same order in which the template titles and fields were created. Data is entered first into the first field created, second into the second field created, and so forth.

At a later date, you may want to enter data in a different sequence. For example, instead of entering a name first in a card, you may want to be able to enter a ZIP code first. (When entering data, On-File places the cursor in the appropriate field for you — you can't independently select the field in which to enter data.) *MultiMate Advantage II* provides an easy method of changing the order in which data is entered — *resequencing* using the Enter and Home keys.

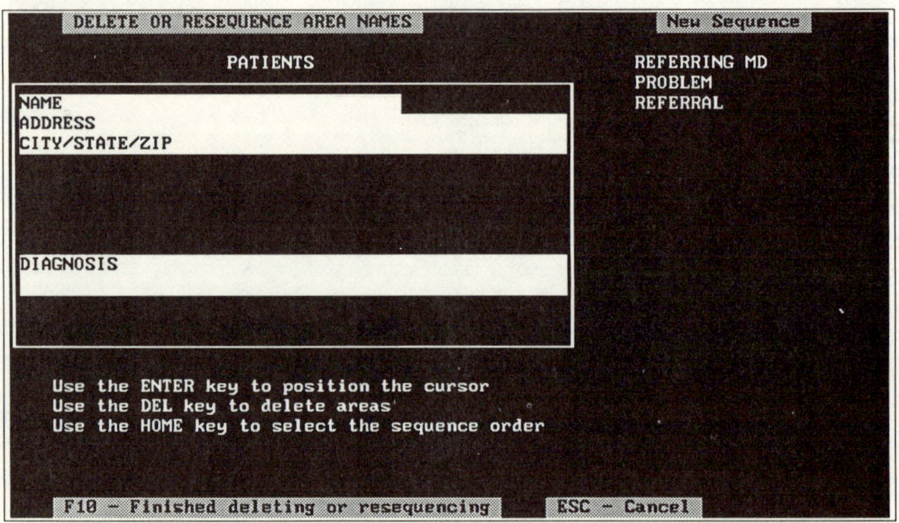

Figure 13-9. Delete or Resequence Screen

Note: Resequencing does not change the order in which the fields appear on the template. Rather, it changes the order in which the data is entered into the fields. (It also changes the order in which columns are printed when creating a report using a template.)

To resequence the order of entering data:

• Press F3 from the Edit Existing Templates screen.

- Use the Enter key to move the cursor to the area (field) in which you want to enter data first.
- Press the Home key when you get to the desired field.
- To the move the cursor to the area in which you want to enter date second:
    Use the Enter key.
- To select that field:
    Press Home.

Repeat the process for all the fields. You'll notice that as you do this, the fields will be removed from the card and will appear in ascending order on the right hand side of the screen, which allows you to see exactly what the order of data entry will be. You'll need to go through all the areas or fields; then, press any key to continue.

Delete a Field

Deleting is accomplished using the Resequence screen.

To delete a field:

- Call up the Resequence screen, as described earlier.
- Use the Enter key to move the cursor to the area you want deleted.
- Press the Del key to remove the area.

To save the deletions:

- Press F10

Rename an Area or Field

You can rename an area or a field using the Edit an Existing Template screen.

To rename an area or field:

- Press F2 from the Edit an Existing Template screen.
- Enter the new name.
- Press F10. (Enter saves the original template name.)

Copy a Template

Sometimes it's easier to create a new template using an existing one as its base than it is to start from scratch.

For example, if you have a Transmission template and want to create one for engines, the simplest procedure might be to make a copy of the Transmission template and then modify it to suit engines.

To copy a template within the same box:
- Press F4 from the Create and Edit Templates screen.
- Press F4 repeatedly to search through the names of existing templates.
- Press F10 when the template you want to copy is named.
- *MultiMate Advantage II* will now ask you to create a name for the copy. Enter the new name.
- Press Enter. The template has now been copied.

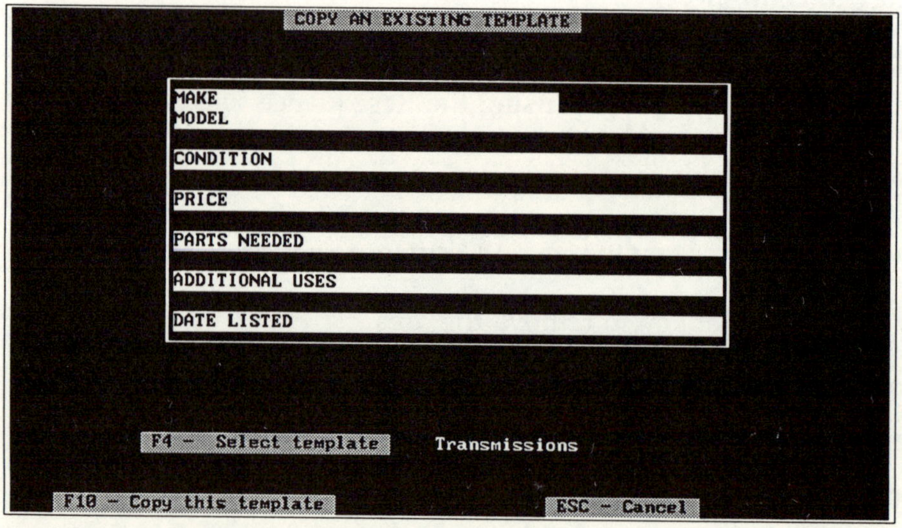

Figure 13-10. Copy an Existing Template Screen

Combine Cards and Templates

Once you have a series of templates, it's quite easy to combine them with your cards.

Create a New Card as described earlier. As soon as the card screen is called up, look at the bottom of the screen where *F3* is highlighted—you'll see the current template selection (the selection may be *No Template Selected*).

To switch to another template:

- Press F3.
- Press F3 repeatedly to rotate through all the templates available in the current box.
- Press F9 when you find the template you want. This will put the selected template on the card.

Enter Information Using a Template

The data you enter is not directly entered onto the template; rather, it will be on the lower portion of the card. The area you first enter data into will be either the first area you created on the template or the area you resequenced to be first.

To enter information:

- Type in the data.
- Press Enter. This enters the data directly into the card and automatically moves you to the next area where you can enter more information, and so forth.

Copy a Template to Another Box

If you have a template that's in one box, but you really need to use it on cards in another box, you have two options: You can create a new template in the second box based on the one in the first box; or, you can copy the templates in the first box to the second box.

While copying may seem the simpler solution at first, it involves certain problems—the most significant of which is that when copying templates between boxes, the templates that are copied into the target box *overwrite* (destroy) any existing templates in that box.

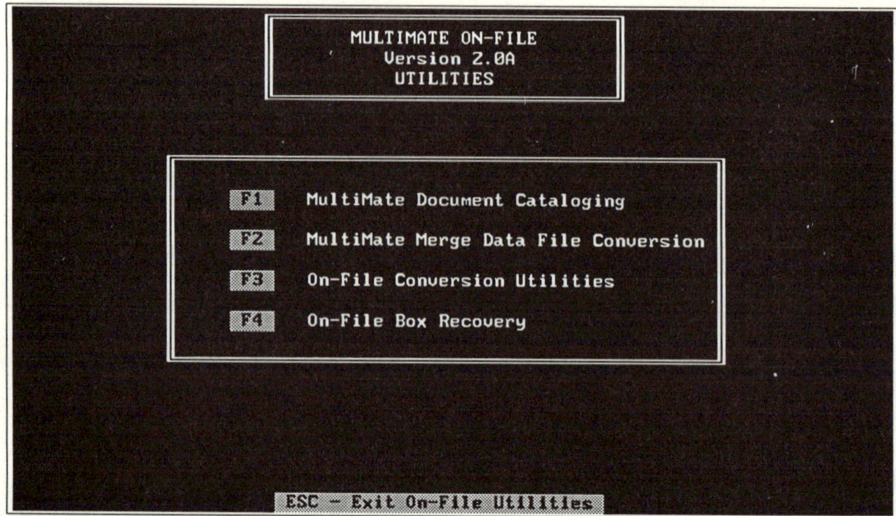

Figure 13-11. On-File Utilities Menu

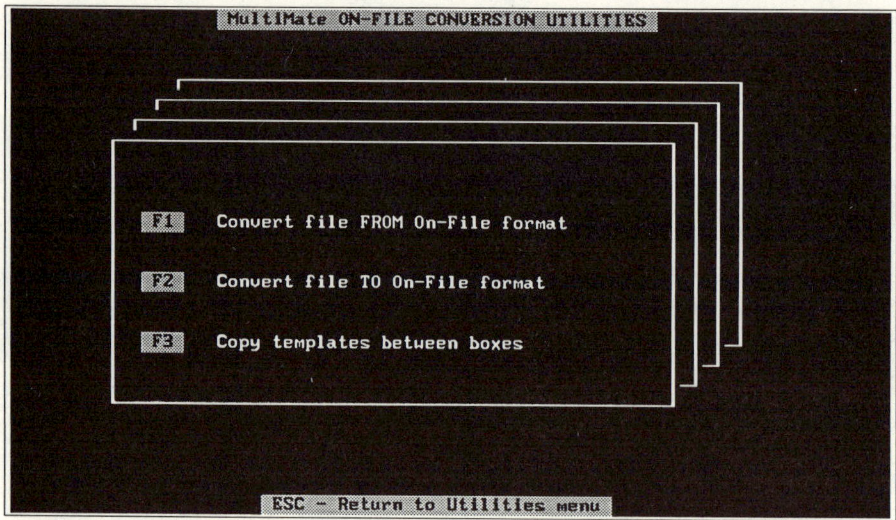

Figure 13-12. On-File Conversion Utilities Menu

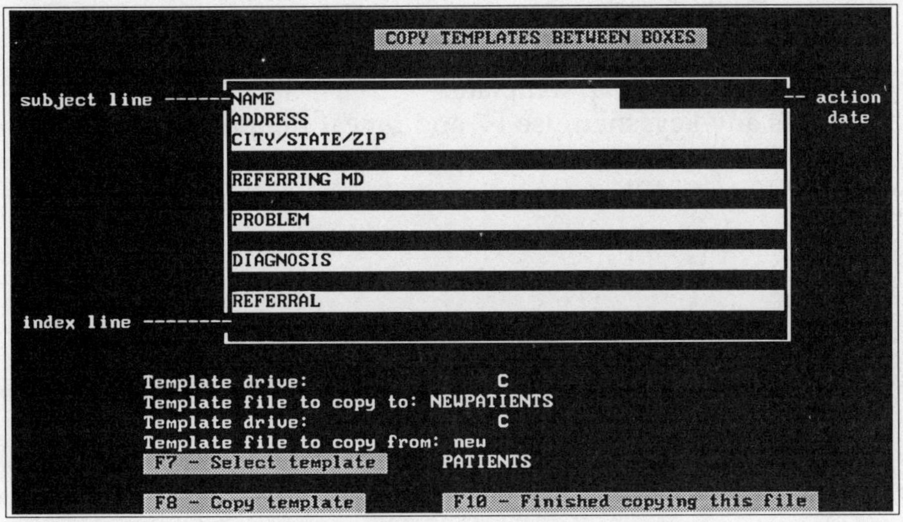

Figure 13-13. Copy Templates Between Boxes Screen

**To copy one or more templates from an existing box
to a target box:**

- Exit On-File and return to the *MultiMate Advantage II* opening
  screen.
- Select On-File Utilities (4).
- Select F3 until you get to the Copy Templates Between Boxes
  screen.
- Indicate the drive and box you want to be the target.
- *MultiMate Advantage II* will respond by asking if there is already
  a template file in the box. If your answer is *Yes,* you overwrite
  (lose) all the templates in that file. (If you want to save the templates, you must first copy them to an empty box, using this
  procedure.)
- Indicate the drive and box from which you want to copy a template.
- *MultiMate Advantage II* responds by offering three options:

F7	Select template
F8	Copy template
F10	Finish copying this file

- To indicate the template you want to copy:
  Use the F7 key. Repeatedly press F7 until the name of the
  template you want appears.

- To copy the template:
    Press the F8 key.
- To copy an additional template:
    Press any key; then use F7 and repeat the previous process.
- Press F10 to end the copy process.

> **TIP:** If you have a box in which resides a large number of templates and you want to copy a new one into that box, sometimes it's easier to make a printout of the template to be copied and then re-create it in the box. Remember, when you copy even one template into a box, it overwrites all the existing templates in that box.

Sorting and Searching Through Cards

Thus far we have concentrated on the creation of cards in our card box—we've been concerned with entering data. The real power of On-File, however, is its ability to manage data once the information has been entered into the boxes.

In the following section, you'll learn how to sort, search for, and extract data from the cards in the boxes. The first step in the procedure is to identify those cards with which you want to work. This is called *searching and selecting*.

To begin Search and Select:

- Select F2 from the main On-File menu to call up the Search and Select Cards menu.

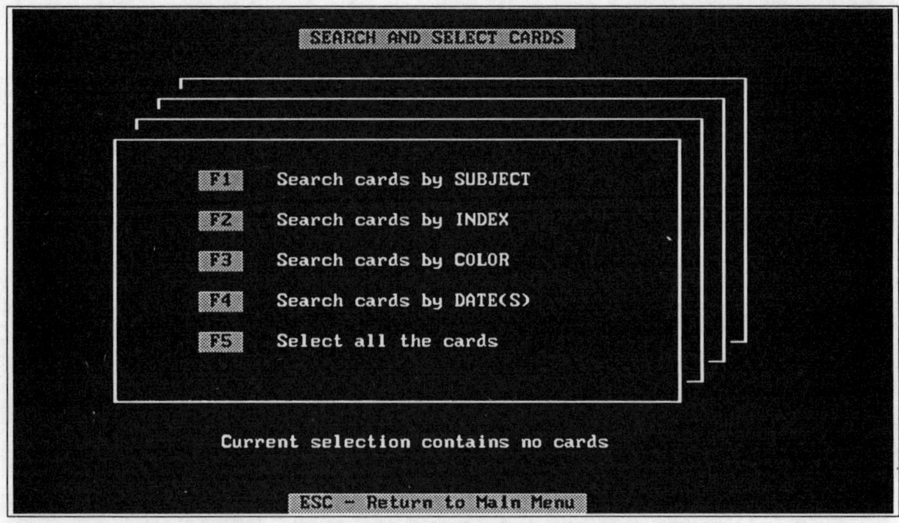

Figure 13-14. Search and Select Cards Screen

This screen allows you to create a "deck" of cards. The number of cards you've selected to be in this deck is indicated at the bottom of the screen. If you haven't yet selected any cards, the screen will read CURRENT SELECTION CONTAINS NO CARDS.

You can search for and select cards by

- Subject (Subject Line)
- Index (Key words on the Index line)
- Color
- Date(s)

The procedure is relatively simple and is similar for each method of searching.

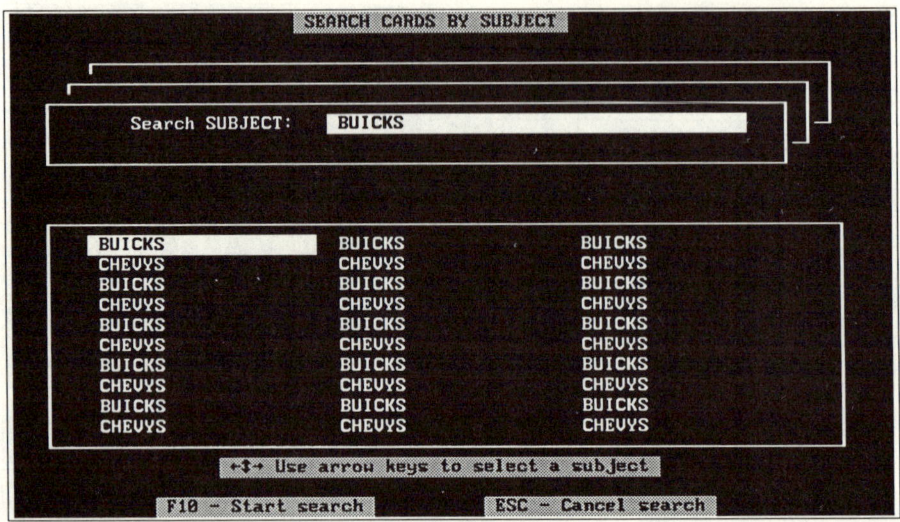

Figure 13-15. Search Cards by Subject Screen

To search by subject:

- Press F1 to call up the Search Cards By Subject screen.
- This screen lists all the subjects you previously entered into your cards; the right and left arrow keys allow you to scroll through the entries.
- Press F1 to highlight the subject you want to search for.

On-File immediately conducts the search. The cards that are found are put into a scrap file under the Create and Edit Card Selection screen, where you're able to work with them.

To search by key words in the Index:

- Press F2 to call up the Search Cards By Index screen.
- This screen lists all the key words you previously entered into your Index line; the right and left arrow keys allow you to scroll through the entries.
- Press F1 to highlight the key word you want to search for.

On-file immediately conducts the search. The cards that are found are put into a scrap file under the Create and Edit Card Selection screen, where you're able to work with them.

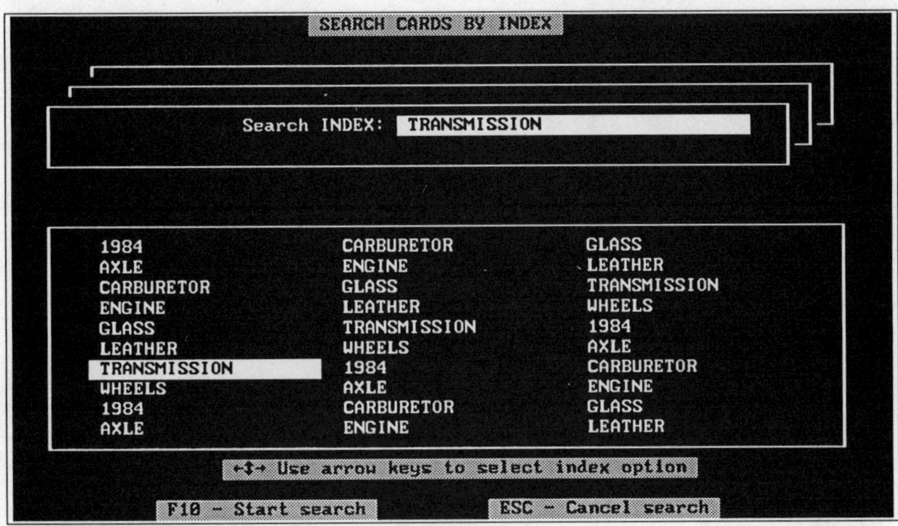

Figure 13-16. Search Cards by Index Screen

To search by color:

- Press F3 to call up the Search Cards By Color screen.
- This screen lists all the colors available.
- Press F1 to highlight the color you want to search for.

On-File immediately conducts the search. The Search By Color method simply extracts all cards of a particular color and, in some ways, is the simplest of the search procedures. The cards that are found are put into a scrap file under the Create and Edit Card Selection screen, where you're able to work with them.

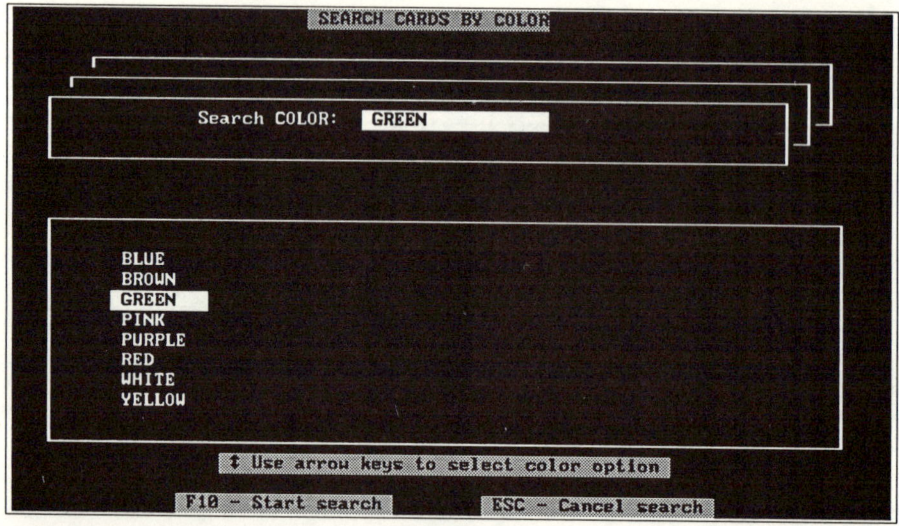

Figure 13-17. Search Cards by Color Screen

To search by date:

- Press F4 to call up the Search Cards By Date screen.
- This screen asks you to enter the range of dates you want searched.

Figure 13-18. Search Cards by Date(s) Screen

To search for a single date:

- Highlight the Single Date selection.
- Enter the date.
- Type all dates as MM/DD/YY.

To search for a range of dates:

- Highlight the Range selection.
- Enter the date range in which you want On-File to search.

To search for before/after dates:

- Highlight either the *All dates before* or the *All dates after* selection.
- Enter the date.
- Press F1 to begin the search.

The cards that are found will be put into a scrap file under the Create and Edit Card Selection screen, where you'll be able to work with them.

To select all cards:

- Press F5.

This selects all cards in the box and creates a scrap file with all the cards in the box. The scrap file can then be used for copying and other file management procedures. (See the section on file management later in this chapter.)

Matching Selected Cards for a Word or Phrase

This powerful tool doesn't appear onscreen as an option until you've first selected one of the other options (F1–F5) on the Search and Select Card Screen. When Match Selected Card for Word or Phrase does appear, it allows you to search for a perfect match. Using this command, you can extract a single card that may match another card.

To begin the match function:

- Press F6 to call up the Match Selected Cards for Word or Phrase screen.

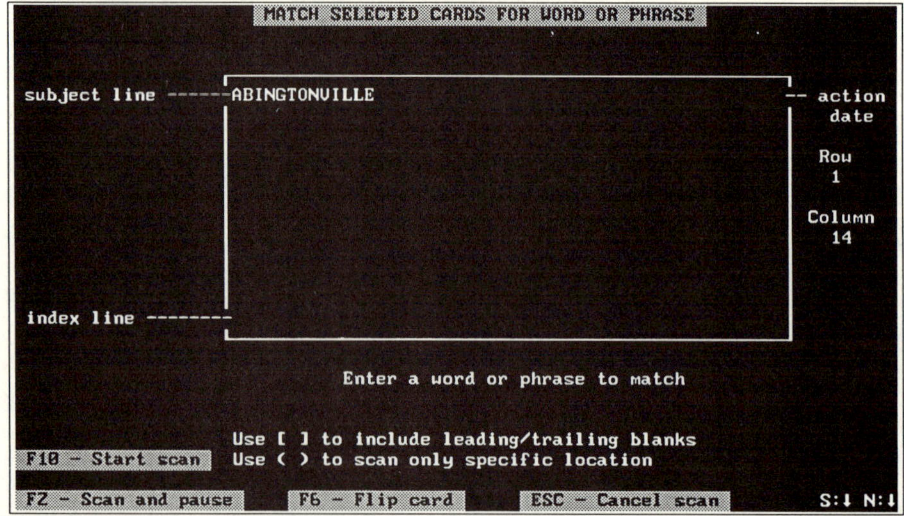

Figure 13-19. Match Selected Cards for Word or Phrase Screen

To search for a match:

- Write in the characters *exactly* as you want them matched. For example, if you type in *Muffler,* the program will search through all the cards for the word *Muffler.*

To flip the card:

- Press F6.

To limit the search to a particular area:

- Place parentheses around the word—in this example, (Muffler)—to search for the word only on the line on which you've written it.
- Place brackets around the word—[Muffler]—for the search to include leading and trailing blank spaces.

To search the entire deck:

- Press F10.

To pause at each match and display it onscreen:

- Press F2. After matched cards are found, the Build a Card Selection menu appears.

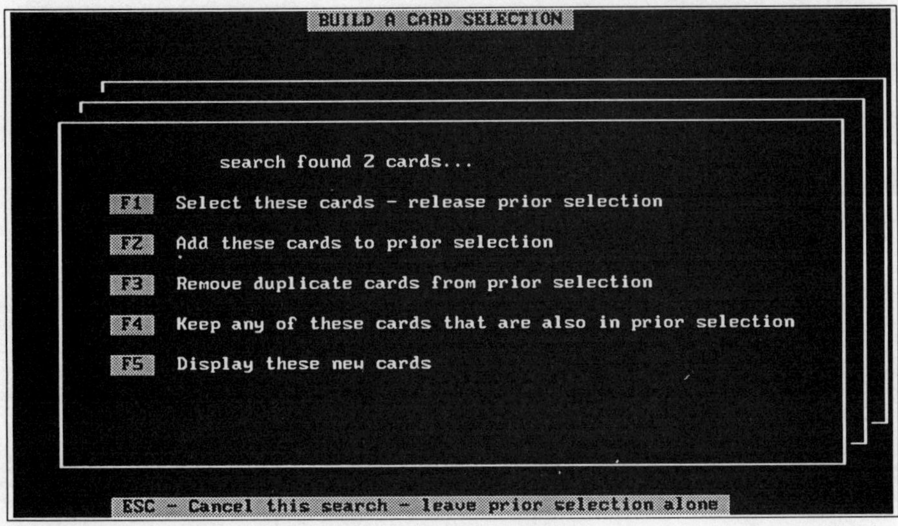

Figure 13-20. Build a Card Selection Screen

The Build a Card Selection menu tells you how many cards were found in the search, and then gives you specific options regarding how to handle the cards, summarized as follows:

F1	Substitute the current cards for the previous selection.
F2	Add the current cards to the previous selection.
F3	Remove cards duplicated in the current and previous selection.
F4	Compare the current and previous selections and keep duplicates.
F5	Display the new cards found.

Pressing F1–F4 returns you to the Search and Select Cards menu for additional searching. Pressing F5 brings up the Temporary Display of Cards Screen (Figure 13-21).

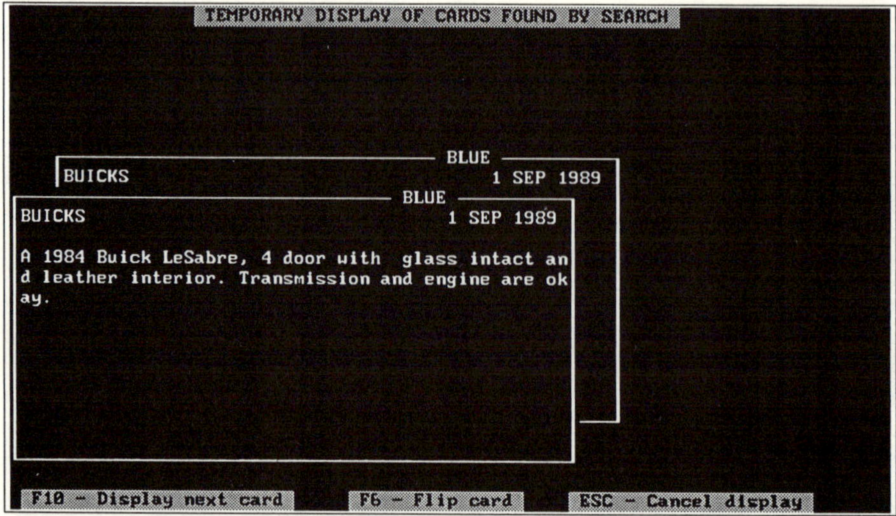

Figure 13-21. Temporary Display of Cards Found by Search Screen

To view the cards you selected in your search:

• Press F5. You can now see which cards have been selected.

To display the next card:

• Press F10.

To toggle between the front and back of the card:

• Press F6.

To return to the Build-a-Card Selection screen:

• Press Esc.

Sorting, Editing, and Printing Cards

The Search and Select feature allows you to extract cards from a file box. Once they're extracted, you can manipulate them in other ways, including sorting, editing, and printing.

We'll consider editing and sorting here; printing will be covered separately. The various functions are from the Display of Current Card Selection screen. This screen contains all the cards you selected in your Search and Select procedure.

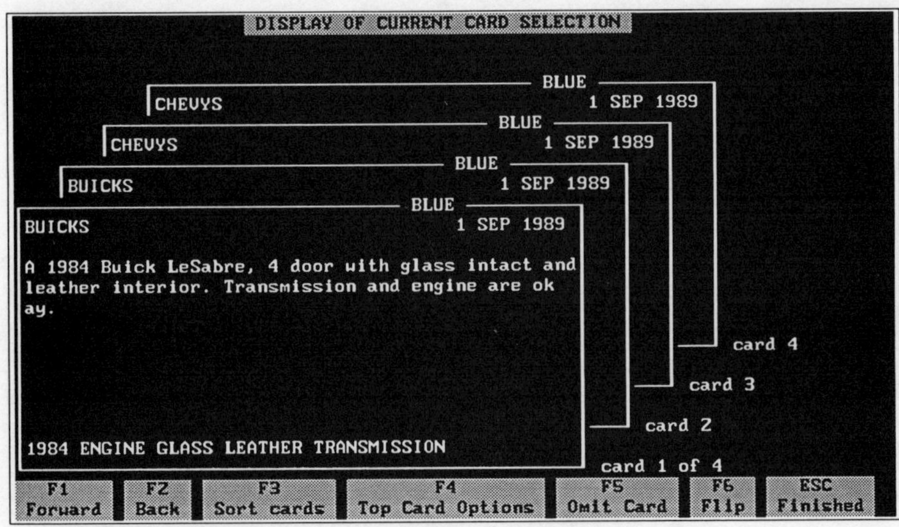

Figure 13-22. Display of Current Card Selection Screen

To move forward through the list:

• Press F1.

To move backward through the list:

• Press F2.

To flip a card:

• Press F6.

To escape:

• Press F10.

We'll now consider the two remaining options: Sort Cards (F3) and Top Card Options (F4) in greater detail.

Sorting Cards

Sorting allows you to easily arrange the cards in a selection in either *ascending* or *descending* order.

To activate Sort:

• Press F3 from the Display of Current Card Selection screen to call up the Sort Cards Screen.

187

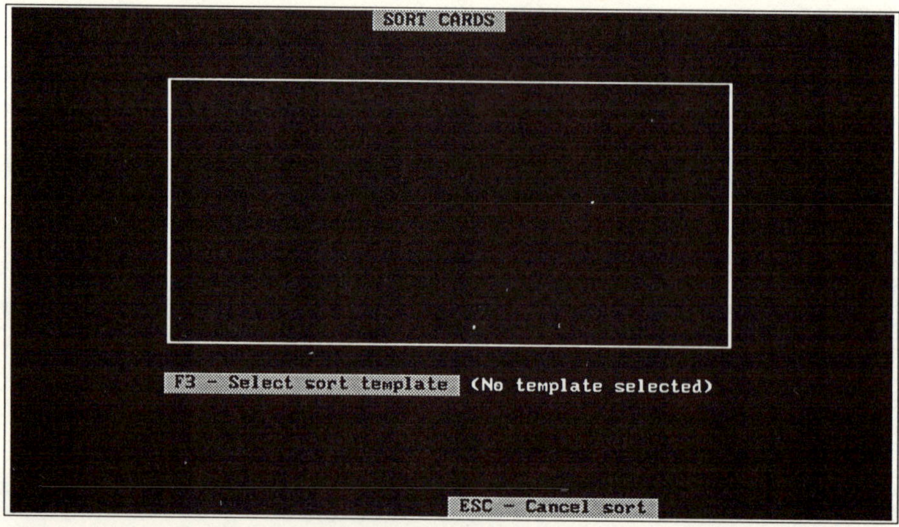

Figure 13-23. Define Sort Cards Screen

Note: Since On-File sorts by fields, you must have a template made in order to use this function. Also, you can only use this function after you've conducted a Search and Select and have produced a card selection.

To select a template:

• Press F3. (Press it repeatedly to call up the various templates available.)
• Press F10 to call up the Define Sort Cards Screen.
• Use Enter to move through the various fields.

To activate *Ascending* Sort:

• Press F3.

To activate *Descending* Sort:

• Press F5.

To activate Sort:

• Press F7.

To begin the sort:

• Press F10.

To cancel the sort:

• Press the Esc key.

Editing Cards

You can edit and print cards as well as perform other functions by selecting Top Card Options, which allows you to examine an individual card (the first one) in your selection more closely.

To activate Top Card Options:

• Press F4.

Note: In the Display of Current Card Selection screen, you can change the top card by using F1 to move forward in the deck and F2 to move backward in the deck.

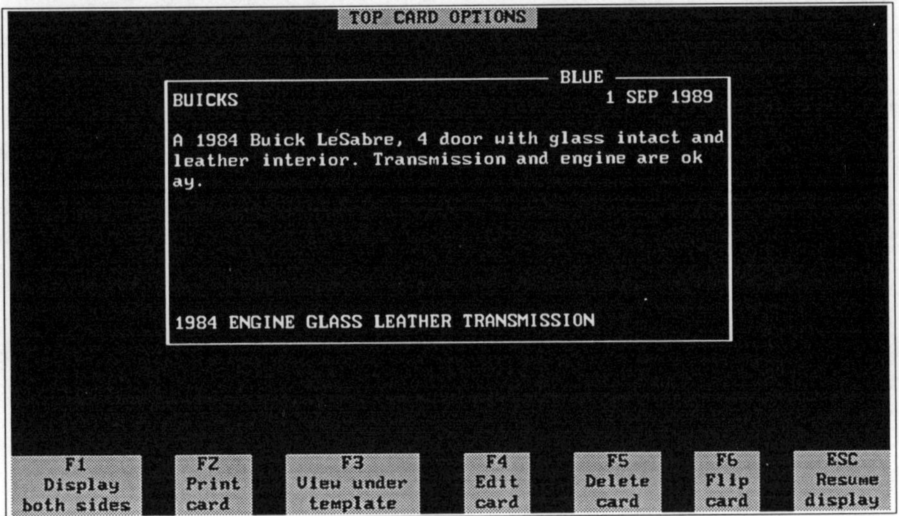

Figure 13-24. Top Card Options Menu

To see both sides of the card at once:

• Press F1.

To quick print the card:

• Press F2.

To flip through templates:

• Press F3

To edit the card:

• Press F4. This is essentially the same edit menu discussed for editing cards.

To delete the card:

• Press F5.

To toggle between the front and back of the card.

• Press F6.

To cancel:

• Press F10.

These, then, are the basic data managing tools you have with On-File. They allow you to manipulate the card records in a variety of ways so you can extract almost any kind of information you need.

There are also other management procedures that can be performed with On-File, which we'll now consider.

Printing Cards

In the previous section, you learned how to "quick print" an individual card as part of the Top Card function. Now we'll see how to print with more versatility.

To access On-File's print function:

• Select F4 from the main menu.

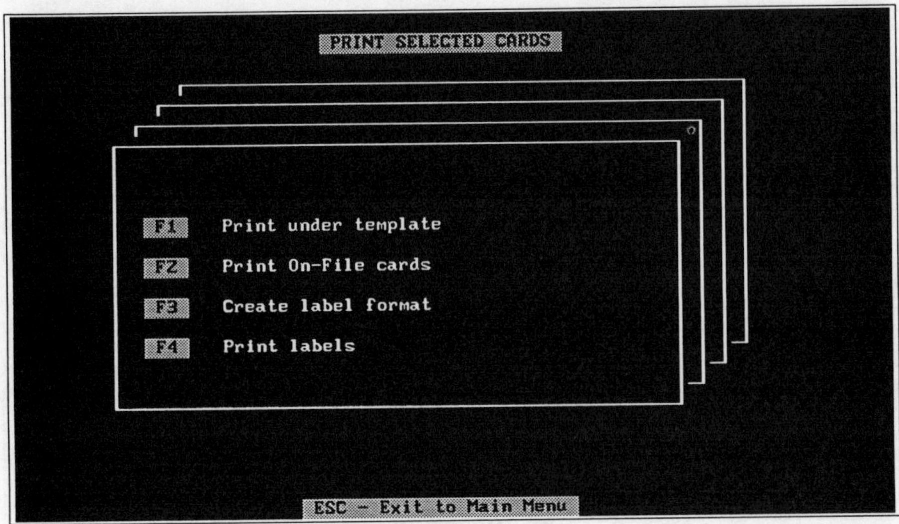

Figure 13-25. Print Selected Cards Menu

In order to print cards, you must have first selected them (as just described). In addition, the print results you get will depend on the printer you're using. With LaserJets, you may find that vertical spacing doesn't correspond to the code sent by On-File. A bit of experimenting should quickly allow you to determine your printer's capabilities.

Note: For those who have basic programming skills, you can send the correct codes to almost any printer by using BASIC. The code sequence and method of creating the BASIC program are normally contained in the printer's documentation. Unfortunately, there is no easy method of sending code to the printer through On-File. (On-File does NOT send an initialization code to the printer, so any setup commands you send through BASIC will apply when On-File is accessed.)

To print under templates:

• Press F1. On-File prints out the information in your card selection.

The card data is printed out in the order in which it was entered on the template and is printed in "run-on" style (paragraph form) at 80 columns.

To print:

• Press F1.

To select a different template:

• Press F4.

To select vertical spacing:

• Press F9; 1 is single space, 2 is double space, 3 is triple space; higher numbers indicate additional lines of spacing.

To exit:

• Press F10.

> **TIP:** As noted earlier, you can set up your printer prior to entering On-File by using BASIC. For example, through BASIC you can send the codes for condensed or extended type.

To access the Print On-File Cards screen:

• Select F2 from the Print Selected Cards menu.

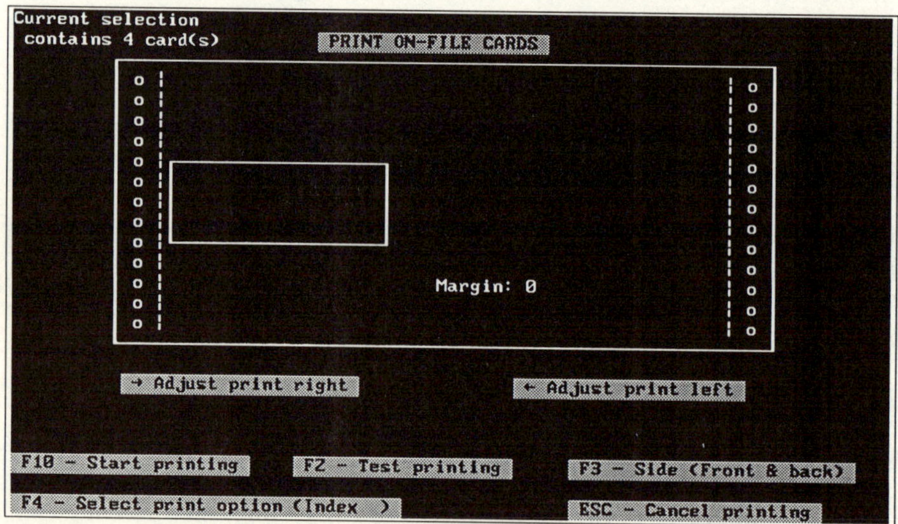

Figure 13-26. Print On-File Cards

The screen depicts form-feed paper and shows the location of the card. By default, both sides of the selected cards are printed in a 3 × 5 inch format on 8½ × 11 inch paper.

To move the location of the printout on the paper:

• Use the left and right arrow keys.

To see where the cards will be printed on the paper:

• Press F2 and a test pattern will appear. You can then make adjustments as necessary.

To print the front only, the back only, or both the front and back:

• Press F3.

To print either the front or back on an 8½ × 11 inch format or a 3 × 5 inch card format:

• Press F4 (This is a toggle switch.)

To cancel the print:

• Press F10.

Printing Labels

Printing labels with On-File is easy because of the graphics displays. You can see onscreen exactly what you're going to get from the printout.

Note: You can only print labels after you've made a card selection.

Create a Label Format

To print labels, you must first create a *label format,* which is simply a description of how you want the labels printed. You can have only one label format per box at a time and only one template per label format.

```
                    CREATE LABEL FORMAT

        NAME
        ADDRESS
        CITY/STATE/ZIP

        REFERRING MD

        PROBLEM

        DIAGNOSIS

        REFERRAL


        F3 -  Select template       PATIENTS
 F10 - Create using this template          ESC - Finished with create
```

Figure 13-27. Create Label Format Screen

To activate the Create Label Format screen:

• Press F3.

This screen allows you to flip through the various templates included in the box to see which one will form the base of the label format.

To flip through the formats:

• Press F3.

To select a template as a basis for the label format:

• Press F10

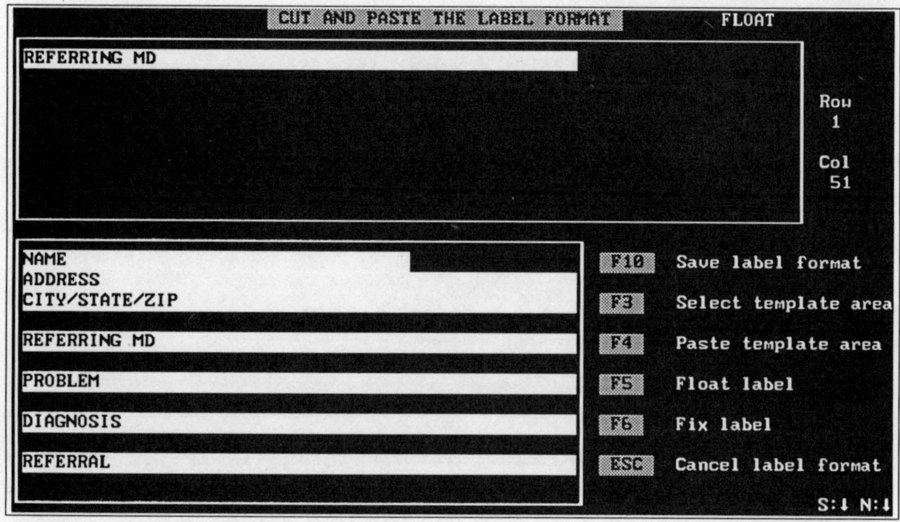

Figure 13-28. Cut and Paste Label Format

As soon as you select a template, the Cut and Paste Label Format appears. This screen has two boxes. The top box contains the future label, the bottom box contains the chosen template. (If the top box is full, use the Del key to empty it.)

The procedure involves moving areas from the template to the label format; areas in the template blink.

To flip through all the areas of the template, allowing each to blink:

• Use the F3 key.

The arrow keys move the cursor in the label box (top). Move the cursor to the position where you want the blinking area in the template to be printed.

To select an area in the template to be copied to the label format box:

• Press F4.

Repeat the process until all the areas have been copied to the label format box.

To create blank spaces:

• Use the space bar.

Float and Fixed

After you've created the label format, you have the option of printing the format exactly as it appears (Fixed) or removing blank spaces and closing up text (Float).

To Fix text:

• Press F6.

To Float text:

• Press F5.

> **TIP:** Try both Fixed and Float the first time. The results will vary with each format so you won't really know which you prefer for your label until you see the two compared.

To save the label format:

• Press F10

To print labels:

• Select F4 from the Print On-File Cards menu.

You may select the location of the labels to be printed both vertically and horizontally.

To adjust horizontal placement:

• Use the left and right arrow keys.

To adjust vertical placement:

• Use the + and − keys.

To run a test pattern to see placement:

• Press F2.

To hand feed individual sheets:

• Press F5.

To use continuous feed:

• Press F5. (Repeatedly press F5 until the proper mode comes up.)

To pause between labels:

• Press F6.

To start printing:

• Press F10.

To stop printing and readjust:

• Press F9.

To cancel printing:

• Press Esc.

To skip a label:

• Press F5.

Special Features

On-File offers several features. You've already seen Create and Edit Templates; now, we'll cover the remaining features.

To call up the Use Special Features screen:

• Press F5 from the main menu.

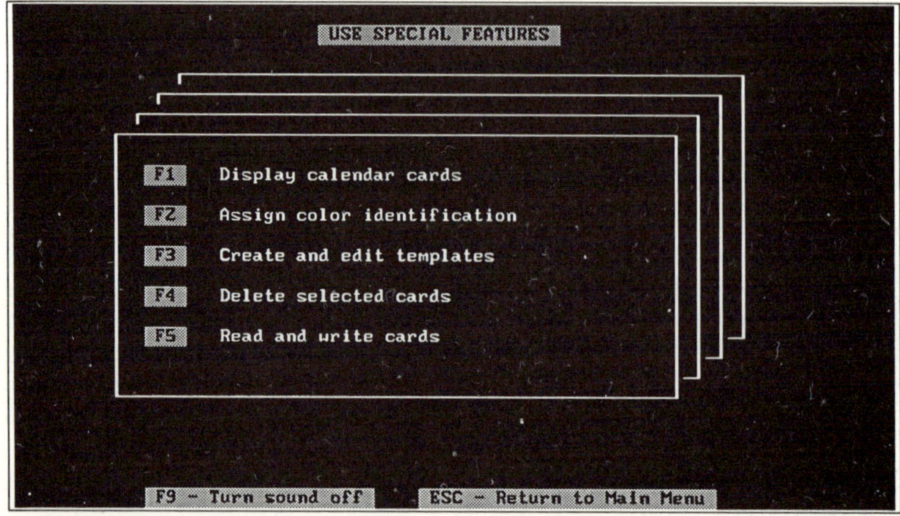

Figure 13-29. Use Special Features Screen

Calendar Cards

This is a useful calendar function.

To call up the calendar function:

• Press F1 to call up the Display Calendar Cards screen.

To look at the month ahead:

• Press F1.

To look at the previous month:

• Press F2.

To look ahead one year:

• Press F3.

To look back one year:

• Press F4.

To repeat the process:

• Hold down any of the function keys on the Display Calendar
Cards screen.

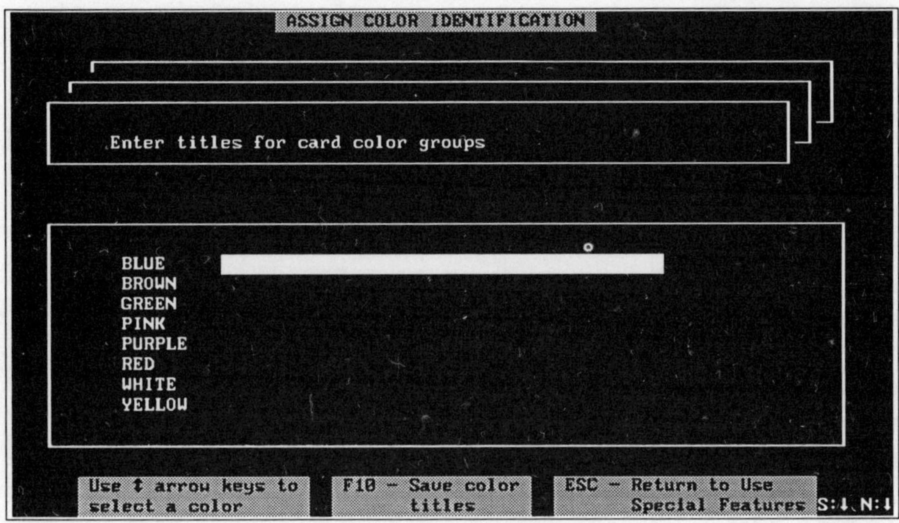

Figure 13-30. Assign Color Identification Screen

Assign Color Identification

To call up the Assign Color Identification screen:

• Press F2.

With this function, you can assign titles for each color group. For example, all blue cards could be dental records, all brown cards hospital charts, and so forth.

To select a color:

• Use the up and down arrow keys.
• Enter the title (up to 40 characters).
• Press F10 to exit and save.

Delete Selected Cards

You can delete the cards you just selected using the Search and Select feature.

To call up the Delete Selected Cards screen:

• Press F4.

To delete cards:

• Select *Yes*; you will lose the cards.
• Select *No*; you will escape without any changes.

Card Management

MultiMate Advantage II provides a facility for transferring cards into and out of On-File. You can transfer between *MultiMate Advantage II* files and ASCII files. You must have previously selected cards as described earlier.

To write to a file:

- Press F1.
- Give the drive and the file name (or box name) of the selected cards.
- Press Enter.
- Give the name of the destination file.
- Press F10.

To read from a file:

- Press F2.
- Give the drive and the file name (or box name) of the selected cards.
- Press Enter.
- Give the name of the destination file (or box).
- Press F10.

Write to a *MultiMate* Merge Data File

You'll recall from earlier chapters that a Merge Data file allows you to print merge with a document file. You can use the cards from On-File for the Merge Data file, thus allowing you to create instant mailing lists or other lists.

To write to a Merge Data file:

- Select F5 from the Use Special Features menu to call up the Read and Write Cards Menu.
- Select F3 to create a Merge Data file. *MultiMate Advantage II* will respond by indicating the number of cards in the selected deck.
- Press F3 to select a template. (You must use a template for this operation.)
- Press F10.
- Give the drive and name of the new Merge Data file.

You can create automatic file-numbering by making the last character of the filename a number. If you do this and the cards selected are too large to fit in the file, On-File will automatically create a new Merge Data file with the same name as the original, only one number higher. For example, if the first file is called NAMES1, the second file will automatically be called NAMES2, the third will be called NAMES3, and so on.

Write to a *MultiMate* Document File

You can also write directly to a *MultiMate Advantage II* Document file. The text will be divided into one page for each record. The advantage of using this function is that you don't need to use a template as you did when writing to a Merge Data file.

To write to a Document file:

- Press F5 from the Read and Write Cards menu.
- Press F10.
- Give the drive and then name the new document file (you can use the automatic file-numbering just described.)

Write to an ASCII File

ASCII files are universally read by other programs. You can use this facility to transfer On-File material to a format that can be incorporated into database or word processing programs.

To be useful, however, you must indicate file delimiters and other information so when the file is read, the relationship of fields and records can easily be determined. This is accomplished by using a template.

To write to an ASCII file:

- Press F4 on the Read and Write Cards menu.
- Use F4 to select the template.
- Press the F10 key.
- Indicate the drive and then name the new ASCII file.
- Press Return.

On-File Utilities

On-File contains several utility programs, which are reached from the *MultiMate Advantage II* opening menu.

To call up the On-File Utilities menu:

- Select 4 from the opening menu.

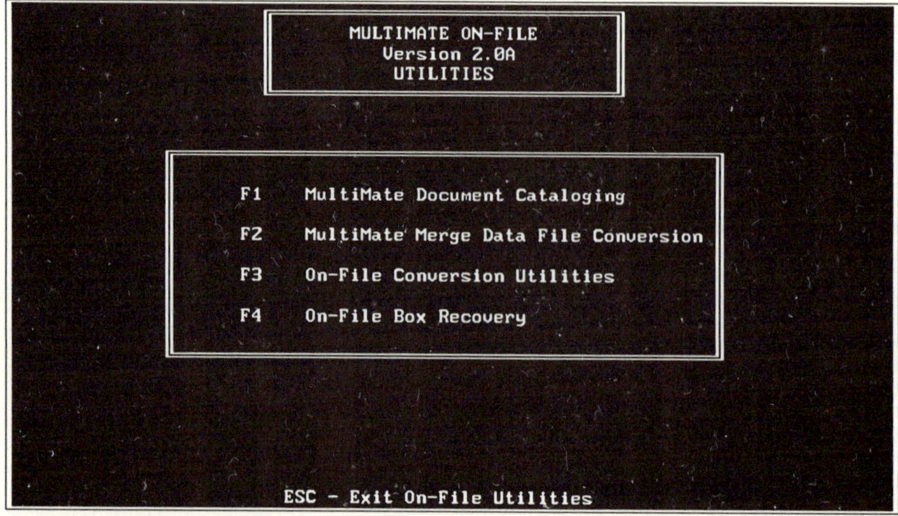

Figure 13-31. On-File Utilities Menu

Document Cataloging

This utility allows you to use the power of On-File to catalog your *MultiMate Advantage II* documents. It uses the information on the document summary screens to prepare cards for each document. These cards can then be searched and sorted in the usual fashion. Of course, to use the document summary screen, you need to use special templates which come prepared in the MLIBRARY file.

To use this program, you must copy the MLIBRARY file to the box in which you want it to function.

To copy the MLIBRARY file using the DOS commands:

- Exit On-File and get to the DOS prompt.
    From a hard disk system:
    Type C:\MM\MLIBRARY. * C:\MM\BOXNAME. * (assuming MLIBRARY is on the subdirectory C:\MM.)
    From a double disk drive:
    Put the Utilities disk in drive A and the Document disk in drive B.
    Type COPY A:MLIBRARY. * B:BOXNAME.*.
- Call up *MultiMate Advantage II.*
- Press F4 from the main menu to engage the On-File Utilities menu.

Perform Document Cataloging for a Subdirectory (Or Disk)

This transfers data from Document Summary screens to On-File cards. It also allows you to update data from summary screens.

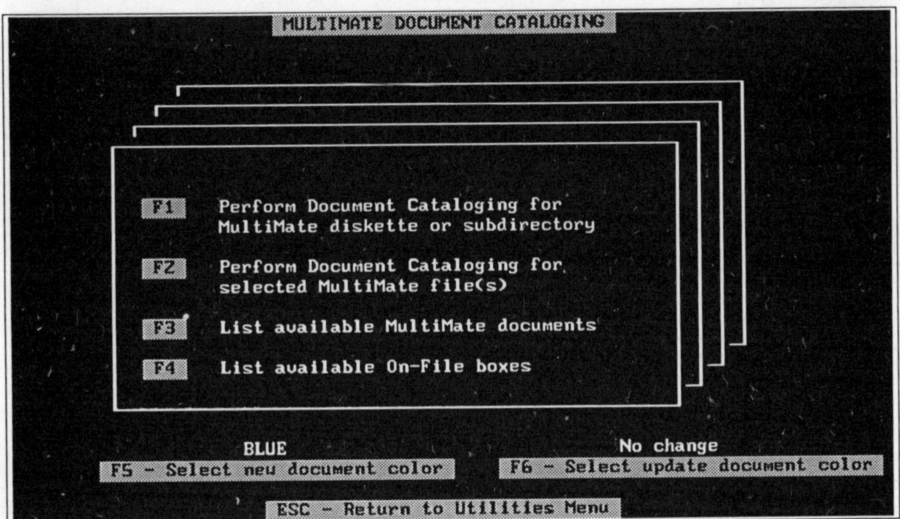

Figure 13-32. MultiMate Document Cataloging Screen

To perform document cataloging for a subdirectory or disk:

- Press F1 on the On-File Utilities Menu to call up the Document Cataloging screen.
- Use the F5 and F6 keys to select the colors for your new and updated cards.
- Press F1.
- Give the drive that has the box with your cataloging templates (the MLIBRARY file you just installed.)
- Give a box name where you'll store your new cards.
- Give the drive and path indicating where your *MultiMate* documents are kept. (Or give the drive where the data files are located.)
- Name the subdirectory where the templates will reside. (*MultiMate Advantage II* creates a special subdirectory for these templates.)

The program responds by calling up the Document Cataloging screen and indicating the *number of cards found, the number of documents found, the number of new documents found to be added,* and *the number of documents not found to be deleted since the last update.*

To update the catalog:

• Press F10 .

Edit the Cataloging Process

You can now control what happens during the cataloging process.

To delete all extra cards:

• Press F10
• Select *Yes*; if you answer *No,* the editing process will begin.

To review the cards:

• Press F2 .

To scroll through the template titles:

• Press F3 .

To save a card:

• Press F5 .

To flip a card:

• Press F6 .

To delete a card:

• Press F10 .

To exit:

• Press Esc.

Perform Document Cataloging for Selected *MultiMate Advantage II* Files

This utility allows you to update or add document cards.

To perform document cataloging on selected files:

• Select F2 from the Document Cataloging Screen.
• Give the drive where the card box to be updated or to be added to is located, and give the card box name.
• Give the drive and name of the document.
• Indicate the name you gave to the disk or subdirectory in the installation process explained earlier.
  The updating process is now engaged.

List Available Documents or On-File Boxes

To list available *MultiMate* documents:

• Press F3.
• Give the drive that contains your *MultiMate Advantage II* documents.
• Press F10. *MultiMate Advantage II* responds by listing the documents on that drive.
• Use F1 to switch drives.

To list available On-File boxes:

• Press F4.
• Give the drive that contains the On-File boxes.
• Press F10. *MultiMate Advantage II* responds by listing the On-File boxes.
• Use F1 to switch to another drive.

Merge Data File Conversion

This conversion allows you convert data from a *MultiMate Advantage II* Merge Data (list) file into a file that can be read by On-File.

The only tricky part about this conversion is that you must create a template in On-File that matches, field by field, the areas used in your Merge Data file. If the fields aren't matched, the data is deleted from the new cards. One card is created for each record.

Figure 13-33. Merge Data File Conversion Utility Screen

To convert a Merge Data file:

- Press F2 to call up the Merge Data File Conversion Utility screen.
- Fill in the data required onscreen:
    On-File Drive
    On-File Box
    Merge Data File Drive
    Merge Data File Name (excluding the extension)
    Output File Drive
    Output File Name

MultiMate responds by calling up the Data File Conversion Screen and displaying the template selected.

To select a different template:

- Use F3.

To select a color:

- Press F4 .

To convert:

- Press F10.

On-File Conversion Utilities

This conversion allows you to convert an entire file to an ASCII format or from an ASCII format to an On-File format. It's particularly useful when you want to insert a list document generated by another program into On-File.

To call up the On-File Conversion Utilities screen:

• Select F3 from the On-File Utilities menu.

Converting To and From On-File

To convert *from* On-File *to* ASCII:

• Press F1.

To convert *to* On-File *from* ASCII:

• Press F2.

To copy templates:

• Press F.

When you press F1 or F2, you're asked to give the source and target drives and filenames. Onscreen instructions specify where to put the On-File drive and name, and the ASCII drive and name.

To begin the conversion:

• Press Enter.

TIP: Certain rules apply when converting from ASCII to On-File. In general, these rules require that the ASCII file corre spond to the parameters of On-File, including the following:

• To be identified, fields must appear within open and close quotation marks.
• The fields themselves should be separated by commas.
• The first field must contain the name of an On-File color.
• The second field must have a date and must be 50 characters in length, including the date.
• The subject cannot be more than 35 characters in length.

(Continued)

(Continued)

> • No field can be more than 50 characters in length.
> • The record should be 25 lines in length, including front and back.
>   For more information, see Chapter 11, "Converting Files."

Copy Templates Between Boxes

You can use this utility to copy as many cards as you want from one box to another. The important thing to understand is that the copying process automatically destroys (erases) any templates in the target box. If you want to save those templates, first copy them to an empty box.

To copy templates between boxes:

- Press F3 from the On-File Conversion Utilities menu.
- On-File responds by asking a series of questions:
    Target Drive?
    Target Box?
    Replace Existing File With That Name? (You must answer *Yes* in order to copy, but this will erase any existing templates in the target box.)
    Box containing templates to be copied? (Give the first template filename and press Enter.)
- You're then given three options.
    To select a template:
        Press F7.
    To copy a template:
        Press F8.
    To exit the utility:
        Press F10.
- Press *No* to exit; press *Yes* to begin the process over again.

Box Recovery

You may be able to recover a box which was somehow damaged so it can't be opened.

To recover a box:

- Press F4 from the On-File Utilities menu. On-File attempts to read the damaged box and write the recoverable data to a new box.
- Type the drive and name of the damaged box.
- Type the drive and name of the new box. (Do not add an extension; On-File will automatically add the .MOF extension.)
- Press Enter.

On-File responds by attempting to write as many cards as possible from the damaged file to the new file.

TIP: Try running the Box Recovery utility several times. Each time you may get different results, some better than others.

After you've created a recovered box, you'll need to go through the process of converting it to an On-File box. Simply use the "opening a new box" procedure (outlined earlier) and then copy the recovered file into that box.

You may also want to delete the damaged box files once you're sure you can't recover anymore data from them. Use the DOS ERASE commands.

This completes the tour of On-File—a natural companion to *MultiMate Advantage II*. Use it whenever you have significant data you need to manage.

Installing

Installing *MultiMate Advantage II* is neither a difficult nor time-consuming operation. Those familiar with computers can probably accomplish the installation in just a few minutes. If you're new to computers, however, and new to *MultiMate Advantage II*, it can be confusing. In this appendix, you'll receive hints and tips for making installation as quick and painless as possible.

MultiMate Advantage II is shipped with both 3½-inch and 5¼-inch disks. The installation for both sizes is similar—the major differences being between those who install on a hard disk and those who use the program on a double floppy drive computer.

Recommendations

While you can run *MultiMate Advantage II* on a double floppy drive computer, you'll be much happier running it on a hard disk drive. To use added features like Spell Check requires more memory than is usually available in RAM, once the program is loaded. Thus, on a double floppy drive system, you'll spend a lot of time switching disks.

XT or AT?

MultiMate Advantage II is a *page-oriented* program, which means it saves each page as you type to permanent memory. This can substantially slow down the program as you move between pages.

For an 8088-8086 chip machine (PC/XT) this can mean anywhere from four to seven seconds of waiting time while *MultiMate Advantage II* saves the last page you typed. On the other hand, if you use an 80286/80386 machine (AT or higher), the waiting time is reduced to a second or two. The time difference may not seem like much, but it can be a factor when you're in the middle of a document, wanting to get through it.

RAM (Random Access Memory)

In order to run *MultiMate Advantage II*, you need an IBM or clone that runs MS-DOS (or OS/2). While the program will run on earlier versions, you're recommended to use MS-DOS 2.0 or higher.

Your computer needs a minimum of 384K of free RAM. Since hidden files take up some RAM, you should have more than 400K to be safe. A typical configuration is 512K of RAM.

Note: MultiMate Advantage II *is a sensitive program, and unless your clone has a high level of compatibility, the program may either not run properly or not run at all.*

Monitor

You can run *MultiMate Advantage II* with virtually any type of monitor. The onscreen display, however, will differ depending on the type of monitor you have.

For example, with a monochrome monitor, you'll actually see the underlining of words onscreen. With a color monitor, you won't see the underlining of words; instead, you'll see a color (or black) pattern where underlining will appear when the document is printed.

Graphics

MultiMate Advantage II incorporates substantial graphics capabilities, including line and box drawing, shaded lines, and other features. If you have a graphics board (CGA/EGA) and a color monitor, all the graphics available will be displayed onscreen.

If you don't have a graphics board and you're using a monochrome monitor, you may not be able to see the graphics that are available from *MultiMate Advantage II*.

Printer

MultiMate Advantage II will work with virtually any printer on the market; however, the quality of the print as well as attributes (such as boldfacing, fonts, and so on) will differ depending on the abilities of the printer used.

Generally speaking, you can expect the following results:

Impact Head (Daisywheel)	Letter-quality attributes are limited to features like underlining and boldface.
Dot-Matrix	Draft-quality (near letter-quality with some printers); all print attributes; several different fonts (roman, italics, enlarged, condensed, and so on).
Laser Printer	What you get will be determined entirely by the fonts you have available.

See Chapter 8 for more information on printers.

Installation

The installation procedure requires several steps:

- Create subdirectories and a configuration file.
- Run the ID program.
- Copy the disks (make working copies or copy to hard disk).
- Select the printer.
- Begin the program.

Since the procedure is somewhat different for hard disk users and floppy disk users, we'll consider each separately.

Hard Disk Users

You must have DOS installed on a subdirectory before you begin installing *MultiMate Advantage II*.

To create a DOS subdirectory:

- Get to your root directory.
- Type CD\.
- Type MD\DOS to create a DOS subdirectory.
- Copy your DOS files to the subdirectory.
- Place your DOS disk in Drive A.
- Type COPY A:*.* C:\DOS.

This will create a subdirectory for your DOS files.

To create a subdirectory for MultiMate Advantage II:

- Get to the root directory (CD\).
- Type MD\MM.

This creates a subdirectory, off your root directory, called MM. (You can use a different name, but MM is easy to remember.)

Create a path from the *MultiMate Advantage II* subdirectory to the DOS subdirectory. (See your DOS instructions.)

Finally, you need to configure (or reconfigure) your operating system to handle the memory requirements of *MultiMate Advantage II*.

To determine if you have a configure file already established:

- Get to your root directory.

- Type CD\.
- Press Enter.
- Type DIR CONFIG.SYS.
- Press Enter.

If you have the configuration file, it will be noted; if not, a message will tell you FILE NOT FOUND.

To create a new CONFIG file:

- Get to your root directory (CD\).
- Type COPY CON CONFIG.SYS.
- Press Enter.

This creates the configuration file. Now you have to give it the memory requirements. In earlier versions of *MultiMate,* this consisted of a statement such as FILE = 15. For *MultiMate Advantage II,* you now need to add the following:

- Type FILES = 20.
- Press Enter.

To close the file:

- Type CONTROL + Z.
- Z will appear onscreen, indicating that you've hit the correct keys.
- Press Enter.

Now reboot your computer. When it's rebooted, it will automatically read the new configuration file and be ready to receive *MultiMate Advantage II.*

To modify an existing CONFIG file, you need to add or change the FILES = 20 statement, yet retain whatever other statements are in the configuration program (since they may be used by other programs on your system).

To find out what's in an existing configuration file:

- Type TYPE CONFIG.SYS.

This displays the configuration file on your screen. While this file is still displayed on your screen,

- Follow the procedure just given for configuring a file.
- After you've typed the line FILE = 20, retype all the other statements in the configuration file.
- End as above with CONTROL + Z.

To run the ID program:

- Place the boot disk in Drive A.
- Type A: (this takes you to Drive A).
- Type ID.
- Follow the onscreen information. The answers you give will be displayed each time this version of *MultiMate Advantage II* is called up.

Now enter the new MM subdirectory and begin copying the *MultiMate Advantage II* disks to it.

To copy the disks:

- Type A: (this takes you to Drive A).
- Type COPY *.* C:\MM (this copies all the files in Drive A to Drive C and the MM subdirectory.

5¼-inch disk users:

- Copy the boot disk.
- Copy the System disk.

3½-inch disk users:

- Copy the boot disk.

To install the printer:

- Place the printer disk in Drive A.
- Type A: to go to Drive A.

To run the printer installation program:

- Type PRINTER. The printer installation program will appear.
- Follow the instructions onscreen.

Now copy the rest of the program to the *MultiMate Advantage II* subdirectory (3½-inch users will have already copied the utilities files, which are incorporated on the printer disk). You need to copy the following:

- Dictionary and thesaurus disks
- Utility disk
- Conversion disks
- Other disks

You don't need to copy the On-File disks until you plan to use the program. If space is a problem, you may also leave off the Conversion disks and the Dictionary/Thesaurus disks; however, you won't be able to run these programs.

To start MultiMate Advantage II:

- Type CD\MM. This takes you to the *MultiMate Advantage II* subdirectory.
- Type MM. The *MultiMate Advantage II* opening copyright screen will appear.
- Press 1 to get started. This will take you to the word processing opening menu.

To create a new file:

- Press 2.

Double Floppy Drive Users

The procedure for floppy drives is similar to installing for a hard disk drive, so references will be made when the same procedures are used.

To begin:

- Run the ID program as described.
- Next, format 10 new disks and make working copies of each *MultiMate Advantage II* disk. The format and disk copy procedures are outlined in your DOS manual.

Typically, the copy procedure involves the following:

- Put the *MultiMate Advantage II* disk in Drive A.
- Put the newly formatted target disk in Drive B.
- Type COPY A:*.* B:.
- Press Enter.

WARNING: If you reverse the order of the disks, you could erase the program. Be sure the MultiMate Advantage II *disks are copy-protected (the notch is covered) and you've placed the disks in the proper drives for your computer before beginning.*

To install for printers:

• Place the working copy of the System disk in Drive B.
• Insert the original Printer disk in Drive A.
• Type Printer and follow the onscreen instructions.

To Create a CONFIG system (or modify an existing one):

• Follow the instructions for hard disk drives with one exception: Put your DOS disk in Drive A and use the A prompt instead of the C prompt.

To start the program:

• Place the boot disk in Drive A.
• Type MM.
• Type 1 when the copyright screen appears.
• Type 2 to create a new file (from the opening menu).

Note: You'll need to enter data on a separate formatted disk placed in Drive B. When you're asked for the drive on which your files are to reside, type B.

Special Considerations

MultiMate Advantage II will not work properly with certain graphics boards; however, the program does include modification files for two of these:

```
STB Graphics Plus II boards              .STB
Compaq Monochrome Graphics Screens .CMP
```

If you have either of these, you must copy the modification files to your WPSYSD.SYS files.

To copy the modification files:

• Type COPY *.STB *.SYS or COPY *.CMP *.SYS.

Upgrading from Earlier Versions of *MultiMate*

To update an existing system (you have two choices):

- You can delete all the old files and install *MultiMate Advantage II* as a new program, or
- You can update existing files.

If you choose to update:

- Be aware that earlier versions did not have the ID program; *you must run the ID program.* (Delete your old WP.EXE file first.)
- You must also run the printer program described earlier.
- Finally, the dictionary is also different for *MultiMate Advantage II.* A conversion program is located on the system disk to convert the old dictionary to the new.

Index